TIME MANAGEMENT FOR A MODERN WORLD

MAKING MANAGING TIME EASIER

MORTON HEWITT

CONTENTS

For my wife Michelle, I dedicate this book to you for the years of strength and unwavering support you have afforded to both our marriage and I. I am truly grateful, thank you.

INTRODUCTION: WHY TIME MANAGEMENT IS IMPORTANT

At one time or another, everyone struggles with time management. It's a universal phenomenon. Whether you're a business executive, a member of a team at work, a college student, or a stay-at-home parent, you have tasks that must be done—most of them on a deadline. What you need to accomplish your tasks and meet your deadlines is good time management.

Poor time management can make many parts of your life rocky. It's not just your business life that suffers. It's also your personal life, your home life, and even your inner life. When you don't manage your time appropriately and well, you can be setting yourself up for failure in so many aspects of your life. You can make yourself—and those around you—miserable. A grouchy husband, an irritable wife, a preoccupied friend, a forgetful son or daughter can all be attributed to problems with time management.

THE EFFECTS OF POOR TIME MANAGEMENT

Without good time management skills, your life can be a total mess. Not only will you not get important tasks done, but you will put unnecessary stress on yourself. That stress can affect both your body and your mind. It can lead to physical health problems, mental health difficulties, and that outcome that everyone wants to avoid—burnout.

Let's start with your physical health. Your body reacts to stress in certain predictable ways. When you're stressed, your body releases hormones such as adrenaline that make your heart speed up, your blood pressure rise, and your muscles tense. This can lead to physical problems such as migraines, insomnia, hypertension, and heart disease. You may eat too much or too little, undermining your general health and affecting your weight. There can even be negative effects on your sex life, too.

Then there are the unpleasant mental effects of stress. You could become tired and irritable, snapping at those around you. You may become anxious, jumping at the smallest things. Or you could become depressed, feeling that you are worthless and that nothing matters. You may be restless and distracted or lack motivation and focus—which can just make your time management even worse and the various aspects of your life less successful.

Of course, the usual remedies for stress—exercise, relaxation practices, good sleep, and nutrition—can help. But good time management skills can help you avoid all that stress in the first place. You won't have to spend your time recovering from stress—yet another thing that takes time to manage! You can make your time productive for the things that really count, like your health and happiness.

Don't forget, though, that stress can take a toll on your business too. Whether you're a sole entrepreneur (with or without employees), a gig worker, a part-timer, a middle manager, or an hourly worker, not managing your time effectively can lead to lost business, lost customers, lost wages, and lost opportunities. Your personal distress puts stress on those around you as well—your peers, your bosses, your team members, your clients, those both above you and below you on the corporate ladder.

There's also a cost to your business, whether you have an Etsy shop managed in your garage or work for a Fortune 500 company. Poor time management can multiply your problems. Say you missed a deadline because you didn't plan properly or gave in to distractions. There's a ripple effect. If you don't get your work done, the next person in line may not be able to meet their deadline either. For example, if you don't turn in the spreadsheet of figures to your team leader, they will be rushed in preparing their presentation to the managers. The whole team will make a bad impression by presenting substandard work.

THE PROBLEM OF BURNOUT

We all know someone who's experienced burnout or even felt it ourselves. Burnout is a major cause of people leaving their jobs—either voluntarily or involuntarily. Burnout comes when you just can't cope any longer, when the bad consequences of poor time management catch up with you.

If you hate going into work every morning and can't wait to get home every evening, you may be on the road to burnout. If your marriage is in trouble because your spouse won't put up with your excuses for staying late at work anymore, burnout may be in your future.

The industries with the highest rates of burnout—up to 70%—are hospitality, manufacturing, healthcare, education, retail, and marketing. Technology, IT services, and finance aren't far behind.

In fact, if you're looking for organizations with a burnout level below 50%, you'll have to look pretty far. Only 15% of companies can claim that statistic (Grucela, 2022).

And what are the consequences of burnout? You could lose your job, your significant relationships, your health, and your peace of mind. It's not too much of a stretch to say that you'll feel like you've sabotaged your own life. In a way, you have, if you've let a lack of time management take control.

WHAT GOOD TIME MANAGEMENT CAN DO

If all these bad consequences can come from bad time management, what consequences come with good time management?

First of all, good time management allows you to focus better. Your mind won't drift off and get you off-track. You won't be bothered with "intrusive thoughts" or random ideas that flood your mind and preoccupy your attention.

Time management is also a good strategy to deal with burnout. Many times, burnout is related to tight deadlines, overwhelming to-do lists, responding to emails and calls day and night, and other causes of a chaotic, unhealthy work environment. Working 60 to 80 hours per week just isn't possible for most people (even if their bosses require it). Good time management can cut those impossible hours down to a more manageable level.

The concept of "time off" seems almost unattainable to most people. It can be difficult to get away from work and relax the way you really need to. Even when they're not actually in the workplace, these people find themselves preoccupied with the minutiae of daily living. They never give themselves a break or simply take a break. Good time management can remedy that. Scheduling effectively also means scheduling for the things you want to do, as much as for the things you need to do. After all, you can't do one without the other. Too much work is unhealthy. Time management cuts down the hours you give to the things you need to do and allows you to give more to the things you want to do—spend more time with loved ones, go to sporting events, take up or rediscover a hobby, or even go on a real vacation.

WHAT THIS BOOK CAN DO FOR YOU

What it really comes down to is this: Do you manage your time? Or does your time manage you? Who's the boss? You or that clock or calendar? When you learn how to structure your time properly, you can once again take control. You'll be better able to solve problems and deal with unexpected crises. You'll react more calmly and perform more efficiently.

This book is written for the person who is sinking under a sea of demands that seem overwhelming and goals that seem unattainable. If you feel like you're drowning all the time at work, at school, or at home, this is the book for you. In it you'll find proven strategies and tactics that can make your life easier through time management.

The first section of the book will take you through why time management can be such an unrelenting, unsuccessful process that can derail you. The second part will focus on how to improve your current circumstances—successful methods for taming the time management monster that eats up so much of your precious time and leaves you exhausted and unhappy.

Along the way, you'll find concrete examples of people from all walks of life who experience time management difficulties, as well as solutions to their problems. You can take these strategies and put them into practice to put yourself on the road to more success, more efficiency, and more effectiveness. Good time management may not be the solution to all your problems, but it *is* a solution that affects every part of your life.

Practice the techniques contained here and see how much

better your life can be! Time management really can improve your life, and this book can help you accomplish it!

WHAT TIME MANAGEMENT
REALLY MEANS

To some people, time management means using a computer program to track their calendar and schedule their time. Computers, alarm clocks, calendars, and even diaries can indeed be valuable tools when it comes to time management. But there are other kinds of strategies that are necessary too.

Let's take a look at some examples of real people's problems with time management to see how the old, tried-but-not-true notions of time management let them down.

CARL'S STORY

Carl is a corporate vice-president at a manufacturing company. He's responsible for many things—approving budgets, chairing meetings, strategizing, and reporting to the executive vice-president and the president of the company on the operation of three departments consisting of two teams each. It's a lot to deal with, but Carl has shown he can handle it. And normally, he can.

Then one day, he was supposed to present an overview of his department's efforts for the previous quarter to the president and the other vice-presidents. When the time came to give his report, though, Carl was not ready. He was put in the awkward position of promising to have the report finished the next week, though he wasn't really sure he could have it ready by then either.

A scheduling program wouldn't have helped Carl. He knew when the report was due and his schedule allowed time for him to prepare it. But during the week before Carl's presentation was due, he was supposed to receive analyses of the operations of the three teams he managed. None of them came in one time. In one case, a department-level manager didn't get his budget reports in when Carl expected them. The reports came in days late, and Carl had to scramble to include them in his presentation.

When Carl had that situation handled, another problem popped up. One of the other departments he supervised couldn't hand in their productivity figures because the leader of that team required hospitalization for kidney stones and no one from his team was able to get the spreadsheets together. That portion of Carl's report was simply missing. The rest of the team had tried to rush through the spreadsheets, but they were unsuccessful.

Carl himself had trouble with his presentation not just because of the missing items, but because the president of the company asked him to prepare an interim report on scheduling problems in his department. Carl knew that he was falling behind on his presentation but felt that fulfilling his boss's request took precedence. After Carl's business lunch with the president, Carl had to rush through the interim report. He had to sacrifice time from his own schedule for that.

Carl was embarrassed that he had to postpone giving his report on quarterly productivity. He knew it was likely to come up in his next evaluation. Carl worked late all the next week in order to hand in the late report. He missed his daughter's soccer game and the company picnic as well.

LESLIE'S STORY

Leslie was a graduate student in microbiology at a prestigious university. Her assignments for her research professor were important, as they related to reactions of various drugs for a range of diseases. Leslie's professor did the actual experiments, but Leslie did the prep work that made the experiments possible. The timing of the experiments had to be precise. Leslie was responsible for preparing the slides of the lab animals' blood work and the solutions that would be used for testing of the animals' blood for parasites that lived for only 12 hours.

One night, Leslie had to stay up late with a friend who was going through a personal crisis. The next morning, she didn't hear her alarm and woke up late. She was late for her first class and missed taking notes on the part of it that she had missed. She spent some time trying to find a classmate who could share their notes with her. She skipped lunch, even though she was diabetic and knew that her blood sugar would dip and make her feel dizzy and weak.

Leslie was late getting to the lab and rushed through her preparations for the day's work. She forgot an important element of one of her preparations and continually dropped beakers and slides because her hands were shaking. She managed to prepare the slides she was supposed to, but barely got them to the professor in time for him to analyze them. Leslie knew he was disappointed in her and probably more than a little annoyed. She worried that it would affect her research appointment next semester. She couldn't get to sleep the next night and experienced the same effects the next day, which added to her worries.

DANIEL'S STORY

Daniel was a counselor in a drug rehab facility, responsible for writing treatment plans for the residents and presenting their cases to the clinical team. His caseload was growing as the facility had just added more beds and was caring for more people.

Daniel was very conscientious. He didn't want to rush through any of the treatment plans because he knew that they were important and affected people's lives. He knew that the clinical team relied on him so that they could put his treatment plans into practice.

One day when Daniel had more treatment plans than usual to work on and had a meeting with the clinical staff the next morning to present those plans, he fell behind on his work. The increase in residents meant that his schedule was pushed beyond its limit. The facility planned to hire more counselors, but they hadn't done it yet. Daniel began working late nearly every night.

On those nights when he worked late, he would call his husband, Roy, at his usual quitting time to tell him when he would be home. Then, two hours later, Daniel would call Roy again and say that he was on his way home. Sometimes he even had to call Roy three hours later to say that now he was really, really coming home. Daniel was exhausted and his husband was losing patience. He wanted Daniel to quit his job and find another one with more regular hours, but Daniel didn't feel he could leave his coworkers and residents in the lurch. But as time went on, he felt more and more burned out and considered quitting.

WHAT WENT WRONG?

Carl, Leslie, and Daniel all had problems that resulted from poor time management—their own or someone else's. They all really cared about doing their jobs well, but just weren't able to accomplish that. All of them suffered unpleasant consequences.

Among the problems that they encountered were not scheduling enough time to accomplish what they needed to, relying on other people's time management and reacting to their problems, and being unable to fulfill unreasonable requests from other people. Their schedules were inflexible or too detailed. They couldn't handle it when their tasks didn't go as expected.

All of their problems had bad effects on their mental and emotional health. Their personal relationships suffered and so did their business relationships. The problems snowballed until there was nothing that could be done to correct them. They suffered from worry, anxiety, embarrassment, and exhaustion.

How much of their problems were caused by poor time management? All of them could have benefited from better time management. In Carl's case, he could have benefited from better time management lower down the corporate ladder, as well as his own. Leslie let a single day with poor time management get away from her until she was terrified of losing her position. Daniel suffered from poor time management that affected his personal life.

None of them could have used standard time management techniques or computer technology to help them achieve what they wanted and needed to. All of them needed to think about time management in different ways and be proactive about managing their time to achieve their goals. They needed to be strategic in their time management.

FLAWS IN TRADITIONAL SCHEDULING

You may think of scheduling as the same thing as time management, but that's not really the case. The way most people schedule their time doesn't take into account factors such as their own natural rhythms of working. They don't expect the unexpected—meetings that run long, personal crises, the ways other people's work affects their own. You can approximate a schedule, but you can never guarantee that it will work as planned.

And that's just scheduling for a day or a week or even a month. Think about your long-term plans. Where do you want to be in life by age 30 or 50 or when you retire? Is it really feasible to schedule whole years in advance, or even the rest of your life? Even if you put intermediate goals in place, what is going to make them achievable when you want them to be? What if your goals, desires, and expectations change and derail the schedule you have already made?

Perhaps you lose that job that was going to take you where you wanted to go. Maybe you encounter a spell of unemployment. How much will that derail your plans? And how can you get back on track? You or a family member could even become seriously ill. Or you might suddenly acquire new family structures when you have to deal with a blended family.

You'll have to react to any of those new situations, and the schedules you've so carefully prepared may simply not work anymore. But is it even possible to manage your time so that unscheduled events can be, if not anticipated, dealt with? Good time management will help you schedule your days, weeks, months, and even years so that you can deal with whatever comes along.

Time management is that powerful.

UNDERSTANDING TIME MANAGEMENT

Time is finite. We all get the same amount of it at the start of every day. Why, then, do some people seem to have control over their time, while others simply don't? The difference isn't in how much time you have, but in how you use it. Time management helps you clear the way for what's really important and set aside what really isn't. It's a matter of priorities, so it's a matter of deciding where you need to spend your time and what can be left for another time. You don't get rid of all your commitments, but you do learn to deal with them proactively.

Time management may sound easy in theory, but it can be complicated in practice. There are a lot of things that can go wrong with a person's time management, as Carl's, Leslie's, and Daniel's stories clearly illustrate. There is not one strategy that would have helped every one of them meet their needs and relieve their problems. There are, however, techniques that each of them could employ to make their burdens lighter. In the next chapters, we'll take a look at some of the things that can get in the way of good time management and strategies that will avoid or negate them.

Time management isn't simply a matter of scheduling, though that's an important part of it. In order to manage your time well, you need to take control—of your time, certainly, but also of your responsibilities, your goals, and your abilities. You may need to make changes in your job, your personal life, your daily routine, or your expectations.

Time management is more than just a one-and-done exercise. It means putting structures in place that will work for you under almost any circumstances, while still being flexible enough to respond to the unexpected—which happens in everyone's lives. Time management means setting up your life and your responsibilities in such a way that your normal daily, weekly, and monthly routines work smoothly. And it means that you can plan for bigger future goals rather than just playing catch-up all the time.

MONITORING YOUR TIME

When you're thinking about improving your time management, the first step is determining where your time goes—what you're doing with the time available to you. Is your time in the morning filled with anxiety over what the day might hold? Do you have to rush to get to work on time? Do you ever forget things that you really need to remember? Is your time at work filled with crises that either you created or that landed in your lap? When you get home in the evening, are you too tired to do more than flop down on the couch and stare at the TV until you finally collapse into bed? And is the next day a dreary rerun of the same old same old?

In order to get control of your time, try keeping a record of how you spend it. Take a single day and write down—or dictate into a digital recorder—the activities that make up your day. Whether it's a typical day or an unusual one, lay down a baseline. Keep this up for a week, if possible. If you have a desk calendar or a computerized one, make note of what actually happened that wasn't in your plans.

Keep making a record after you get home. Do you prepare dinner? Order takeout and wait for it to arrive? Do you have a certain routine to help you unwind, or do you leap straight into dealing with crises at home—whether it's cranky kids or bills that came in that day? Do you still get work-related calls and emails? Do you feel you have to answer them right away? What time do you get to bed? More importantly, what time do you get to sleep?

Was that a typical day for you, or did things happen that were unexpected? Did you notice anything during the day that had a "ripple effect"—one thing going wrong that led to another and then another? Were any of the things that created these ripples under your control?

Next, notice what time of day you seem to get the most done. Are you bright and fresh first thing in the morning, or do you feel logy and unmotivated until after that first cup of coffee or tea? How do you feel on a day when you skip breakfast? Are mid-morning and mid-afternoon your most productive times, or do you work best early in the day and late in the evenings?

Think of your week as well as your day. Are you usually hung over or exhausted on Monday instead of being energized by two days of rest? Do you drag on Friday afternoons or work harder to "clear the decks" for the weekend?

One thing this exercise will do for you is to help you understand your natural rhythms for working, which will help you when you go to schedule your time. Scheduling is not the straightforward subject you may think it is, and we'll talk more about schedules in upcoming chapters but, for now, just map out your day and your week in terms of when you do your best work and when you are more likely to be distracted or less effective.

Of course, if you work an hourly job, a part-time one, or have an unpredictable work week, rather than a nine-to-five salaried one, many of your answers may be different. That's because you probably have less flexibility in when and how you work. Healthcare workers and lawyers are not likely to work 40 hours per week in five eight-hour shifts. Gig workers, sole entrepreneurs, and substitute teachers may have better opportunities to schedule their work when they want to do it.

Still, there are likely to be differences in when and how you work best and most productively based on your natural rhythms. Even factory workers may produce more output in the mid-mornings, once they've fallen into a rhythm than they do near quitting time. Another person in the same job may have a very different natural rhythm. It's different for everyone.

All these factors come into play when it comes to time management.

WHEN TIME MANAGEMENT BREAKS DOWN

There are consequences when poor time management affects your job and your life. Some of them are short-term effects that you can get through with simple changes in how you manage your time.

Others are more significant and can precipitate major life changes. Some affect just you, but others can have repercussions for your whole team, your coworkers, and even your business.

Personal effects of poor time management include feeling overwhelmed, decreasing productivity, and sabotaging your motivation and morale. You can get into a vicious cycle of low motivation leading to poor performance, which leads to even lower morale. That in turn creates more problems of not accomplishing what you need to do, and the cycle continues. When this occurs repeatedly, you get closer and closer to burnout.

Your personal life goes to hell. Your health suffers. You give in to unprofessionalism and damage your relationships with coworkers and customers. You fall victim to lack of priorities and focus. Basically, you sabotage both yourself and the company you work for. You can't be punctual, and you waver between unproductive rushing and putting off necessary tasks.

And all the while this is happening, the business loses productivity, customer satisfaction, and, most worrisome of all, money. How long do you think a business will put up with an employee who costs them all that? How long will the business survive if they don't get rid of people who are liabilities rather than assets?

2

STUMBLING BLOCKS TO TIME MANAGEMENT

Y ou realize that time management is important, but you just don't know how to accomplish it. What is standing in your way? There are a number of hazards that you can fall victim to. They are natural reactions to unpleasant situations, but they can negatively affect your ability to make time management work for you. Some of them are psychological, while others involve not understanding the basic principles of getting things done. Paying attention to which of these time-stealers you fall prey to is the first step in getting past them.

LACK OF AGENCY

"Agency" is the word used to describe the process of taking control of your own life—your actions, your goals, and even your thoughts. It's important in all walks of life, so that you can act rather than be acted upon. Someone who lacks agency doesn't know how to be assertive and how to accomplish the things that will move them forward.

Great leaders have agency and demonstrate it every day. These can be political figures, business leaders, admirals and generals, or even ordinary individuals caught up in momentous events where they find out that they have it within themselves to be heroes. People with agency aren't wishy-washy or timid. They seize the day, get on with the task at hand, and *make* it work out right.

It sounds like agency is a special quality that only a few people have, doesn't it? But that's not true. Everyone needs to have control over their life. Of course, we can't control all the circumstances surrounding us, but we can control many parts of life. For example, a person can control their attitudes. If you approach life with confidence and confrontations with appropriate adherence to basic principles, you are more likely to achieve positive results. You'll be demonstrating your agency over whatever life throws at you.

What does agency have to do with time management? Good time management is one opportunity to demonstrate agency. Too many times attempts at managing time seem to spiral out of control. But a sense of agency will help you take back that control. When you can find a way to not let the problems of scheduling overwhelm you, for example, your time management will be much more effective. You will have taken control over a vital part of your business and personal life.

LACK OF SELF-CONTROL

Related to agency is the notion of self-control. When you lack self-control, you get distracted by the minutiae of everyday life. You give in to distractions such as other people's problems, a constant barrage of emails, and even time spent on social media. Helping other people with their problems, answering emails and texts, and checking news and trends on social media can all be good things, but not if they interfere with your time management plan.

It's easy to let these distractions take over your day. They creep up gradually, eating up your time until you discover it's the end of the day and you haven't gotten anything done. You're putting out fires instead of making real progress.

It takes self-control to tame the many distractions you face on a daily basis. And self-control in turn leads to control of your time—the very definition of time management.

PROCRASTINATION

Procrastination is one of the biggest thieves of time. If you encounter a problem but put off dealing with it, the problem is only likely to get bigger, more complex, and more time-consuming. Suppose, for example, you have a report on your budget due by the end of the day Friday, but you've been putting it off all week. When Friday rolls around, you go into overdrive trying to get it done. But in the meantime, you're neglecting the other tasks that you should have been doing that day and putting them off too. You may get the report in at the last second, but you'll have created a snowball effect. The things you had to put off to get the report done haven't disappeared. They've merely been bumped into another day's tasks.

Why do we procrastinate? Sometimes it's a matter of overconfidence. You think that you'll be able to write that report in two hours, when it will actually take you half a day. You won't have put time for it in your schedule and your time management goes out the window.

Another reason for procrastinating is that the task that needs to be done is unpleasant in some way. You don't want to spend hours poring over shipping schedules because it's simply a tedious chore. So you put it off and then put it off some more. Instead, try seeing it as something you can break down into several parts—scheduling two hours a day instead of doing six hours of it at once—and you'll be better able to convince yourself to do it.

Or you may believe that you work better under pressure—that a tight deadline inspires you to do your best work. That's rarely the case, though. You end up doing a rushed job of poor quality and risk having all your tasks piling up into an unmanageable mess.

Still another source of procrastination is lack of belief in your own ability to write that term paper or prepare those PowerPoint slides. You tell yourself you can't do it, so you don't do it. This doubt can creep into your thinking and become a habit that leads to stress and depression, which make it even more difficult to finish your work on time.

OVERTHINKING AND OVERSCHEDULING

When you overthink things, you make them too complicated to finish. When you overschedule your time, you make it impossible to cram all you need to do into a finite time limit. Both can seriously hinder your time management.

Overthinking has several different effects. For one, you can make a project more difficult than it really is, consisting of more steps than necessary. Even something as relatively simple as planning for a camping trip expands into an endless series of steps. You find yourself trying to think of every eventuality and how to cope with it. You buy a first aid kit for simple scrapes and then start adding items to it in case anyone gets poison ivy or an upset stomach. You set up your tent in the backyard and buy new stakes because one of them is bent. You buy maps of the area in case your GPS doesn't get a signal. You plan every menu for every meal and buy supplies for them. Then you decide you need new pots and pans, a bundle of firewood, and a lighter. Or do you need a propane stove instead? You wonder if you'll need hiking boots and a backpack in case you want to take a hike. You pack clothes for every possible type of weather. By the time you've finished all the planning, shopping, gathering, and trying to anticipate every possible emergency, you've already used a day or two of your planned vacation. Then you spend your time off rushing through all the activities you planned: hiking, fishing, singing around the campfire, practicing your nature photography—and most of all relaxing.

It's easy to see how this can apply to business, education, or housework as well. You end up rushing around, trying to anticipate every possible glitch that might arise, and focusing all your attention on the small details while letting the bigger picture slide. In the end, you eat up the time allotted and find you have only accomplished the early steps of a project.

Overscheduling is similar. You may think you can write a report, schedule workers, take inventory, and order supplies in one week, but can you really? If you've crammed too many things into your schedule for the week, some of them are going to be left hanging until the next week—and messing up your carefully over-scheduled plans for that week as well. In effect, your poor time management snowballs. Your workload appears to increase to more than fill up the time you've set aside for it, and your schedule collapses under the weight of the individual tasks.

"WRITER'S BLOCK"

Just think about writing that proposal for a new product line. You stare at the computer screen, but the empty screen stares back. No ideas come to you. That blinking cursor seems to taunt you. You have no idea how to start, so you don't. You think that maybe rereading that proposal you did last August will give you some inspiration. You talk the problem over with your coworkers, but nothing seems to help. Pretty soon you find that you've wasted the whole morning and still haven't gotten a thing written. Your deadline looms, and you know you won't meet it. That's writer's block.

But you don't have to be doing a written project to experience writer's block. Anything that requires forethought can be affected by writer's block—thinking about what you're going to say at a seminar or even making a grocery list. Your brain whirls with all the possibilities. You lose track of your ultimate goal. Suddenly, it's too late. The seminar has started, or fixing dinner is already upon you. You've wasted your time and have nothing to show for it.

How do writers deal with writer's block? Some turn to another project that they've already started and work on that for a while. If they do that, though, they're only postponing doing the thing that had them so stuck in the first place. And writers usually work on deadlines, so postponing a job can get out of hand too. Jumping back and forth between projects isn't a solution, either. The writer ends up with two unfinished pieces of work rather than just one.

ANXIETY

It's funny. Anxiety can be the effect of poor time management, or it can be the cause of it. Anxiety can either lead to writer's block or be the result of it. Anxiety is a physical sensation—jittery nerves, racing heart, the inability to sit still—but it is also a psychological problem. When you're anxious, you lose the ability to think clearly, to plan, and to strategize. Anxiety of either sort can compound the negative effects of poor time management.

What are some of the consequences of anxiety? Fatigue and poor sleep. Unmet work quotas. Unsatisfying personal life. Stress. And what are some of the causes of anxiety? Fatigue and poor sleep. Unmet work quotas. Unsatisfying personal life. Stress. This pattern makes anxiety tough to counteract. Time management skills can lessen stress and anxiety.

How? Knowing what you have to do and how much time you have to do it enables you to succeed. It lessens anxiety by letting you set realistic goals and know that you have the ability to meet them. When you have that feeling of accomplishment, you have less stress and more motivation to meet those goals. Reducing stress and anxiety is important for both managers and workers, both team leaders and coworkers, and of course, bosses—but also the most basic levels of employees. If anyone falls victim to poor time management related to stress and anxiety, the whole organization suffers. One person who gives in to anxiety puts stress on all the others. Production, efficiency, and morale all go downhill.

Anxiety is a known killer as well. A person with anxiety can get headaches—even migraines. If they're not able to meet schedules because of anxiety, they can decide to skip lunch and make do with a quick snack at their desk or fast food, which increases obesity and all the health problems that can cause. Anxiety can lead to high blood pressure, which can in turn lead to heart disease. People who have constant, untreated anxiety can self-medicate with alcohol or drugs. None of that is good for a person with uncontrolled anxiety or for the organization they work for.

PERFECTIONISM

It's only natural. You want your work experience to be perfect. You want to make the most of your education. You want your personal life to be fulfilling. You want your family to get everything *they* need to succeed as well.

But wait! Life isn't perfect. We all know that. Nonetheless, we strive for perfection in every area of our lives. And it just isn't possible.

Let's take your work life, for example. Expecting it to be perfect is unrealistic. There are always going to be things that are out of your control that will have repercussions. A delivery is late, so you can't fulfill orders. Your biggest client moves their headquarters out of state. You have a health problem and have to take time off work to deal with it.

You may not be able to change any of those things, but you can change what you do about them. Expecting things to go perfectly is not something you can attain. But planning will help you cope, and time management will help you plan.

Expecting things to be perfect can ruin your plans. Trying to be perfect can sabotage your goals. Putting that one last finishing touch on a project may not be necessary—in fact, it may keep you from getting it done on time or at all. You keep seeing tiny flaws that just have to be corrected. You want that document to be proof-read just one more time in case you may have missed a comma or a semicolon here or there. It can cause you to believe that a job isn't good enough unless absolutely everything goes right. And that can lead to stress and anxiety, which we already know isn't something that helps your time management.

Perfectionism is an inability to say, "good enough" and move on to the next thing that will make the various aspects of your life good enough as well. It can tie you up in knots so you can't get anything done. It actually slows down your work and takes you further away from the results you want.

LACK OF PRIORITIES

You probably believe that setting priorities is the key to time management. In a way, that's true, but in another way it isn't. When you set priorities, you say what is important and what isn't. But you may not consider the steps that will lead to making that priority a reality.

Saying something is a priority puts an emphasis on that project, relationship, goal, or other thing you think is the most important. Like perfectionism, though, it may lead you to focusing on that one priority to the exclusion of everything else. You may have heard the saying, "When everything is a priority, nothing is." That's where setting priorities can lead you.

When you set priorities for yourself, you risk making every-thing a priority. Sure, you're a great team member doing an important job, but when you sit down to make yourself a list of your priorities, not everything can be at the top. You'll be dividing your attention between various tasks, including ones that are not as important as other tasks on the list.

It's even more difficult when you aren't deciding your priorities for yourself. Say you work in a small company as an administrative assistant for three different bosses. One insists you take on her projects first. Another puts a job on your desk and says, "Prioritize this." The third one says, "I need this done ASAP." You can't win in a situation like that. If you do take one of the projects as a priority, you're likely to get bad reviews from the other two. If you switch back and forth among the tasks that have been piled on your desk, you risk not getting them all done in time. You've been put in an impossible situation, which causes you stress and anxiety. There's no way to win.

But even setting your own priorities can be a trap. For one thing, your manager may not agree with the priorities you've listed. For another, you yourself may have more priorities—that all need doing right away—than you can reasonably handle. If you don't have good time management skills, there's no way to break the logjam.

IGNORING THE 80/20 RULE

Basically, the 80/20 rule says that 20% of your efforts lead to 80% of your results. In other words, 20% of input is responsible for 80% of your output. It's counterintuitive. You'd think that 20% of your efforts would only lead to 20% of your results, but that's just not so. For example, if you have ten tasks you need to do in a day, doing two of them will provide a bigger benefit than doing the other eight combined.

This equation is also called the "Pareto Principle" for Vilfredo Pareto, an Italian economist who noticed that the 80/20 rule applied to situations as diverse as land ownership (20% of the people in Italy owned 80% of the land) and agriculture (20% of the plants produced 80% of the fruit).

Since the 80/20 rule is so widely applicable, it has repercussions for time management as well. You may find that 20% of your clients are responsible for 80% of your orders. Or 20% of your team meetings lead to 80% of your tasks accomplished. Or even 20% of your coworkers help you with 80% of your projects.

Obviously, you can't just ignore the other 80% of clients, meetings, or coworkers, but you can decide how much time you give to each category. It makes sense to give more of your attention to the factors that give you 80% of the results than to the ones that don't. This is a form of prioritizing that offers great benefits. You maximize your results while minimizing how much time you put in.

3

THE TYRANNY OF TO-DO LISTS

Y ou've undoubtedly written a few to-do lists in your life, thinking that they will help remind you of all the important things you need to do. They may have been recorded on your laptop, penciled in on a scratch pad, or jotted on sticky notes. However, you keep to-do lists, though, they will not really improve your time management skills. You can make a to-do list every day and it still won't help you get everything done. To-do lists are one of the most ineffective ways of managing your time and producing the results you want and need.

You might focus on the items that are easiest to do, for example, just so you can cross something off the list and feel good about taming the other to-dos. (You've no doubt heard the joke about putting "Make a to-do list" as the first entry so you can cross it off right away.) Or you might have items on your list that aren't that easy but require many steps to get done—none of which appear on the list. For example, you might have "Set alarm to go off 15 minutes before the meeting" on your list. It may feel good to cross it off, but how long does it really take you and how much good does it really do? Wouldn't your time be better spent gathering information so that you can be effective at the meeting, or talking with coworkers about what issues they want you to present or solutions they want you to propose?

Take a look at your to-do lists and how they might be hindering you rather than helping you.

MAKING CHOICES

Not all tasks on a to-do list are created equal. It's probably obvious that filing your taxes is more important than planning the menu for the company picnic. But if they both appear on your to-do list, you may be tempted to do the easy one first. You may be fooled by the fact that one will take a relatively shorter time to do than the other. You might therefore think that it will be better to get the smaller one out of the way before you go on to the more difficult one. If you do that enough times, you may find yourself rushing to the Post Office to meet the midnight tax filing deadline or trying to upload your documents when you're too tired to make sure that you have every line and schedule filled in.

One thing that many people overlook in creating to-do lists is whether they must actually complete all the items themselves or whether all of them must be done immediately. Those assumptions can get you tangled up in endless to-dos.

If you're one of those people who feel that things will only be done right if you do them yourself, you'll probably have a hard time taming your to-do list. As noted, perfectionism is a hindrance to good time management. Believing that you have to do everything yourself ends up with you shouldering crushing responsibilities.

What's the solution? Why, delegate, of course! Examine your to-do list to determine what truly are the tasks that only you can do signing contracts for big deals, for example—and which ones can be adequately handled by subordinates, like preparing those contracts. You have to choose what you can realistically do and leave the rest to someone else. That person might even be better able to do the job than you would! And you don't have to delegate to just one person, either—you can have a committee plan the picnic. It's a way of getting buy-in, so they're happier with the results, too.

URGENCY: DO IT NOW OR LATER?

Remember when we said that not setting priorities was one of the major stumbling blocks of good time management? Priorities are very important when you're creating a to-do list or figuring out how to make all the to-dos into "dones." It's important to realize that some tasks should be done before others, and even that some of them must be done *before* you start on others. You need to set up and use a spreadsheet for your expenses, profits, and losses before you file those taxes, for example.

Other ways that you might need to sort your to-do list include creating separate categories or pigeonholes in which to place each item. These might be Urgent Priority, Important Priority, Handle Later Priority, and Unimportant. Or they might be Do By Myself, Get Help With, and Delegate. Those are both more helpful than simply having a to-do list.

TO-DO LISTS AND ANXIETY

What makes to-do lists such problems? They create stress and anxiety, and you know how bad those can be for your physical and mental health. Why add another stressor to an already stress-filled life?

While if you accomplish everything on your to-do list you may feel motivated to do more, you may instead be making yourself more overwhelmed. And if you don't complete everything, you may feel guilty or as if you aren't successful. You might abandon to-do lists altogether, instead of learning better ways to use them.

You might see not accomplishing all of your to-do list as being a failure. Really, though, an uncompleted to-do-list can be the start of the next day's. And if you find yourself repeatedly pushing a task off to the next day and the next, it's worth asking yourself if it really needs doing at all. Maybe the world won't end if you don't do something on Wednesday when you could do it just as easily on Thursday instead. "It'll just be easier" is a valid reason to put off a minor errand, especially if it relieves part of your stress that day.

Anxiety caused by to-do lists, however, can lead to procrastination. You don't want to put off the really important things until the next day. You have to pay attention to what you say "I'll do it tomorrow" about. Think about how long each task will take. If it's a quick one, like refilling the printer paper, doing it tomorrow might not create much of a backlog. Putting off writing your term paper, however, will take considerably longer and can't be put off, since there is a firm deadline.

It's probably advisable to include some anti-anxiety activities on your to-do list, even if they're only small things like going for a walk during your lunch hour or listening to calming music with your earbuds. That way, you'll be accomplishing two things without taking up any more of your time.

THE LENGTH OF TO-DO LISTS

Another reason that to-do lists cause stress is that they're simply too long. You may at first feel more important if you have a lengthy list, but a long list of things you can't get done is not really a recommendation of your ability to accomplish what needs to be done. In fact, it can get in the way.

Experts recommend that your to-do list be no more than four or five tasks long (Kim, 2021). Any more than that and you're probably setting yourself up for failure. A long to-do list can leave you feeling that you haven't accomplished enough if you haven't crossed off every single thing on it. Having too many items on your to-do list can leave you feeling swamped and encourage you to procrastinate. Too many choices might leave you making no choice at all.

Think of a long to-do list as a memory aid, not a time management tool. It reminds you of everything you hope to accomplish. If you have a long list, you can add to and subtract from it as you get things done.

Remember when you were in school and had to memorize a long series of dates and places? You probably studied hard for that test and memorized them by your own system—mnemonics, for example. Then, when the test was over, you promptly forgot all of them. That's because you have what's called "short-term memory" or "working memory," and "long-term memory" or "storage memory." All memory is a way of encoding events in your brain by reinforcing brain cells and their connections as they are used. The longer you need a memory, the more connections your brain makes that reinforce it. If you only need to remember a thing for a short period of time like that list of dates before the test, not as many neurons are activated and the memory disappears quickly.

Your to-do list may be long if you have many things to do, but it can also get cluttered if you include too many short-term items you want to remember. Instead, record just the two or three big things you want to accomplish. Think about the first thing on that list. What are the short-term things you need to do? Prioritize the steps and then make a separate list for those.

For example, you might have "clean the house" as your priority task when expecting overnight or weekend visitors. Your short-term to-do list might include "scrub toilet," "do dishes," and "vacuum floors." Perhaps the last time you had visitors, you forgot to vacuum the floors and were embarrassed by the squashed-down carpet that led from the living room to the kitchen. Once those tasks are crossed off the list, you don't need to think about them and hold them in the front of your mind.

You may remember other house preparation tasks such as "provide clean towels" and "stock up on beer." You'd add them to the shorter list as you crossed off the first things on it. After you'd done all the smaller tasks, you can cross "clean the house" off your major list. The next thing on that list might be "get ready for meeting the new client on Monday." The short-term tasks might be "review our product offerings," "choose a restaurant for the business lunch," and so on. Maybe you don't get all the sub-tasks done by Monday because of entertaining your visitors. Think about which tasks you can do Monday morning, such as making restaurant reservations, and which you must do on Sunday afternoon after the visitors leave, like researching the potential client and their business.

The drawback to this is that you've created two lists. While prioritizing tasks and breaking them down into subtasks may be helpful for getting things done, there are other types of lists you may want to consider.

ALTERNATIVE LISTS

There are other kinds of lists you can make that will help you through your days and weeks besides to-do lists. Try using one or more of them.

Things Accomplished Lists

Instead of making a list of what you need to accomplish, how about making a list of what you've already accomplished? Taking a look at what you've done can be a source of satisfaction and lessen the anxiety caused by having tasks you haven't crossed off your to-do list. It gives you a running list of what you've already gotten done and may remind you of what you have left to do. Or it may give you motivation to keep going and accomplish still more.

A "got-done" list can be a cure for the "I haven't accomplished anything" syndrome. It gives you visible proof that you have indeed accomplished something instead of telling you what you haven't done. It's more satisfying than simply crossing off an item on a to-do list. A computer scheduling program may simply delete a task after you've finished it, leaving you to forget about all you've already done.

The items on your got-done list don't have to be the great, earth-shaking ones, either. Racking up a list of small "wins" encourages you to go on. Just listing "answered five emails" or "picked up books at the library" can give you a sense of pride that will help brighten your mood and carry you through the other things you still have to do. And if you don't get everything done, you can still say, "At least I did 25 pushups today," or "I may not have gotten all the invitations sent, but I made a dent in the pile."

Future Action Lists

You may find that your to-do list is bogged down with day-to-day details—fires that need putting out now. It's important to do those things, of course. But if an idea flits across your mind for something that really ought to be done—sometime, but not right now—keep a list of those things. For example, you might one day think that there has to be a better way of scheduling employees.

Maybe you even have a glimmer of an idea of how to do that. Make a file for that idea. When you hear or see something relevant to it, put that in the same file. Perhaps you see an ad for or an article about a better way of scheduling; stick it in the file or folder for a look later, when you're not all swept up in putting out those fires.

When you finish one big project, look over your "future" files for other ideas to move on to. You might find that some of them are no longer needed—that someone else has been assigned the duty of scheduling and it's no longer up to you, for example. You can delete that file, or you could pass it along to the new person who's doing the scheduling.

You know all those pesky emails that clog up your inbox? There are extensions or add-ons to your email program that "snooze" emails that you just haven't gotten around to. After three days (or however many days), the program reminds you that the email is still waiting. It's a system that prevents less-than-urgent emails from falling through the cracks. They're not exactly on your to-do list, but they're things you might want to address in the near future. They're requests that it's okay to procrastinate on, at least for a little while.

Other Alternatives

Maybe what you need isn't really a to-do list. Maybe instead you need a deadlines list. Sort your tasks by when they are due, with the closest deadlines at the top of the list and the other ones farther down. There will also be "fuzzy deadlines," ones that have some "give" in them. You may want to sort them by the earliest you could reasonably have them done, or by the latest that they can be done by. Just make sure that they show up *somewhere* on your list.

Perhaps the best idea is not to use a to-do list at all, but simply to rely on your calendar—either computerized or the old-fashioned kind. Most of them allow you to mark items with colors or flags, which you can use for "do immediately," "do soon," and "do whenever time allows." Or you can mark hard deadlines in red and soft deadlines in blue. You can even put in intermediary tasks: For example, if you have to finish writing a handbook, you could have "have outline done by," "write proposal today," "proofread," and "deliver" dates included.

4

THE MYTH OF MULTITASKING

The word "multitasking" didn't even exist till the 1960s, when it was used to describe a computer that could work on more than one problem at once. It wasn't a thing that human beings were expected to do. That has changed. Now multitasking is something that is seen as much more demanding than walking and chewing gum at the same time. Now it's considered essential for juggling several tasks at once, even when they each require attention and brainpower. Many companies regard multitasking as essential when considering new hires, and prospective employees almost always include examples of their multitasking abilities in their resumes.

You hear a lot about multitasking in regard to business, but also in terms of "real life." Whether it's a teacher juggling schedules and assignments; a middle manager dealing with multiple emails and phone calls while trying to get a project done on time; or a parent wrestling with the demands of children, spouse, chores, and job, multitasking is something we all think is important in order to cope with modern life.

But is it really? Does multitasking even really exist? And how can it hurt us instead of helping us? Let's look at some of the answers.

BRAIN SCIENCE AND PSYCHOLOGY

What is the brain really doing while multitasking? Science has an answer for that, and it's not good news for multitaskers. The facts say that multitasking doesn't really exist, but that, even if it does, it's not good for business or any other part of life. It makes it impossible to be laser-focused on the most important things.

The brain suffers when you're multitasking. Especially when technology is involved, your brain's gray matter is reduced, particularly in areas that are used "in areas associated with cognitive control and the regulation of motivation and emotion" (Coupland, 2019). The left and right halves of the brain no longer work in sync; they work independently. Multitasking can affect both your working memory and long-term memory. Working memory is essential for accomplishing in-the-moment tasks such as remembering email addresses and passwords, while long-term memory stores more involved events and actions—the results of your last sales meeting, for example.

People who multitask all the time can't filter out what isn't important. They can't manage a working memory. They're chronically distracted. They can't dismiss irrelevant information. Multitaskers' brains try to switch between two tasks that require the same part of the brain—language processing, for example—and end up making more errors than if they did each task separately. *Inc.* magazine reported that "up to 40 percent of productivity could be lost due to task-switching" (Mautz, 2017).

Multitasking doesn't mean that you're actually doing two things at the same time, it means you're switching rapidly back and forth between them. Task-switching is a start and stop process that takes up a measurable amount of time. "It's less efficient, we make more mistakes, and over time, it can sap our energy" (Napier, 2013).

Functional MRI or neural imaging shows that "individuals almost always take longer to complete a task and do so with more errors when switching between tasks than when they stay with one task" (Madore & Wagner, 2019). The multiple tasks place a greater load because the switching occurs among three different parts of the brain's networks.

Psychologists also raise doubts about the possibility and bene-fits of multitasking. The "switching costs" that last for only

a few tenths of a second per switch...can add up to large amounts when people switch repeatedly back and forth between tasks...[E]ven brief mental blocks created by shifting between tasks can cost as much as 40 percent of someone's productive time...Thus, multitasking may seem efficient on the surface but may actually take more time in the end and involve more error (*Multitasking: Switching Costs,* 2022).

In fact, the University of Southern California (2018) reports a study that showed that multitasking actually lowered the IQ by 15 points or so—to the level of an eight-year-old. They add that the shift of attention required for multitasking such as switching from answering email to tracking delivery times and amounts causes the brain to change over from the systems that control language processing to those that govern math processing, leading to inef-ficiency.

WHEN MULTITASKING GOES BAD

The idea of multitasking developed as a way to deal with multiple demands on our time. As the name implies, multitasking is seen as doing multiple tasks at the same time. Talking on the phone while updating a document on the computer is one example. It's supposed to make you more productive by making the most out of the finite amount of time you have every day. It relies on the idea that you are able to split your attention in order to accomplish more than one thing at a time.

Sometimes multitasking seems like a good idea. Who wouldn't want to get two (or more) things done at once in today's fast-paced world? Other times, though, we recognize that multitasking is bad—for example, when someone tries to text and drive at the same time. Driving a car is such a complex task that a person really needs all their attention to do it. Splitting your attention away from all the possible hazards, from simply swerving out of your lane to causing a multi-car crash, is one of the worst ideas that people can try to do.

This form of multitasking is called "distracted driving." Experts say that even talking on a cellphone while driving makes the driver react very much as if they are drunk. Peripheral vision decreases and you lose the ability to anticipate other drivers' actions. A person is better able to split their attention—for instance, listening to the radio—while driving once they are no longer a novice. Inputs such as the position and movements of the hands and feet have become routine.

But there are some inputs that are too much for the human brain to handle: "In fact, driver inattention is involved in about 80 percent of crashes, according to a 2006 study by the National Highway Traffic Safety Administration...Switching modes takes time—maybe only a quarter of a second. But on the freeway, that means you've gone an extra 20 feet before you hit the brake" (Hamilton, 2008). And it's happening a lot. There's "a survey by Nationwide Mutual Insurance showing that 72 percent of drivers say they do other things while driving, like using a cell phone, eating, or drinking" (Parker-Pope, 2008).

MULTITASKING IN BUSINESS

Of course, that doesn't mean that answering an email while talking on the phone is actually dangerous. But inattention there can still lead to mistakes such as hitting "send all" when the email is really meant for one person on a list. It's not life-threatening, but it can certainly be embarrassing and potentially lead to a reprimand at work.

According to *Indeed* magazine, "Multitasking often involves switching back and forth between tasks based on their importance and urgency. For example, answering the phone in a busy reception area while greeting patients or answering emails shows multitasking skills (*Multitasking Skills: Definition and Examples*, 2022). The benefits of multitasking are said to include saving time, saving money, preventing procrastination, increasing brain power, developing resilience, increasing productivity, and conserving resources by reducing the need for hiring new employees. Many articles and books tout the benefits of multitasking.

Multitasking has even been credited with increasing creativity, based on testing students with business simulations and watching contestants on the cooking competition show *Chopped* (UNC Kenan-Flagler Business School, 2020). They proposed that multitasking activates the brain by using both attention and working memory to increase mental flexibility and, therefore, creativity. They noted, however, that this applied only to certain kinds of tasks, primarily those less detail oriented.

Indeed, multitasking is rampant. Clifford Nass, Professor of Communication at Stanford, gives an example: "The top 25 percent of Stanford students are using four or more media at one time whenever they're using media. So when they're writing a paper, they're also Facebooking, listening to music, texting, Twittering, et cetera" (*The Myth of Multitasking*, 2013).

There are jobs where multitasking is a necessity. Nurses, for example, may have to triage patients in the emergency room. Wait staff must keep on top of multiple orders and tasks at a time—greeting customers, taking orders, getting drinks, serving food to different tables. Air traffic control is one of the most multitasking professions there is, and one where multitasking is most essential.

There are other multitasking jobs that are advisable, or even good. Taking notes while attending a meeting or lecture is usually necessary. Taxi drivers must navigate while receiving orders from the dispatcher.

Then, there are jobs and tasks that don't lend themselves so easily to multitasking, though. Working on three different architectural plans at different stages of completion is a bad idea. Managing social media accounts while answering emails is not something a person can easily do. Working on a grant proposal while advising students about their career choices is something no one can—or should—do.

WHY MULTITASKING ISN'T HELPFUL

Multitasking at work is bad for business when you can't focus deeply on the one most important thing, such as connecting deeply with a client or remembering the name of someone you've just been introduced to. Multitasking leads to more mistakes, which can mean the difference between profitability and unprofitability or between safety and accidents.

Even more troubling is the fact that multitasking leads to anxiety. Someone who is multitasking is usually always worried that they're not accomplishing enough or that they may be missing important steps in a process. And we know what anxiety can lead to—physical problems such as high blood pressure and emotional problems such as depression.

Then there's the problem of "flow states" or being "in the zone." These occur when a person is focused on a task, particularly a challenging or engaging task, to the exclusion of everything else. Being in the flow state is a method of getting an enormous amount done and done effectively. If you have a hard task ahead of you and get into a flow state, the time just flies by. Distractions seem to drop away. The flow state is an amazing phenomenon when it occurs—however, being in the flow state can't occur when you're multitasking. In fact, multitasking prevents you from achieving it.

Among the factors that create the flow state are clear goals, focus on a specific task, sense of agency, the bringing together of action and awareness, and a task that is rewarding in and of itself. It's not easy to achieve—you usually can't bring it on by trying to. But you have very little chance of achieving a flow state, with all the benefits it brings, if you are trying to multitask. In some ways, the flow state is the exact opposite of multitasking! Getting rid of distractions and focusing intently are recommended, rather than trying to split your attention.

The flow state is valuable in many areas of life besides business. When you're pursuing a hobby—creating a model train layout or making jewelry—you can get into a flow state and not even realize you're missing dinner. Meditation is another way to experience a flow state.

But don't get the idea that flow state is something you can only achieve alone. It's possible for an entire team to work in a flow state together, working practically in synchronization. Julia Martins (2022) has this recommendation for a team that wants to "go with the flow":

Create working blocks or group sessions where you can all focus on a project, together. Not only will you experience the benefits of being in the flow, but you can share those benefits with your entire team for maximum efficiency and effectiveness.

GETTING AWAY FROM MULTITASKING

Defeating the myth of multitasking can be done in a number of ways. Lin Grensing-Pophal (2022) recommends that you break up your time into separate "chunks," rather than trying to take on more than one at a time. Reserve a time on your calendar for answering emails, for example, and a separate chunk of time for listening to a podcast on customer service or sealing a deal, for example. These chunks of time don't have to be hours long, as flow states might be. In 20 minutes, you may be able to get done a specific task before you go on to the next. In fact, it may be better to get a lot of little tasks out of the way before you start a larger one, so that they don't keep interrupting you.

Bianca Barratt (2019) has several recommendations for getting rid of multitasking. Unfortunately, one is another time management strategy that just doesn't work: making a to-do list. Others may be more effective. Barrett says, "unless you genuinely need to be on hand for something in particular, assign certain periods of the day to check your inbox and then turn off notifications the rest of the time." She also advocates turning off your phone—or putting it away in another room or a locker—to keep you from scrolling through social media.

Of course, for many people, this isn't a good solution, or even possible. If you're a parent, the daycare center or school needs to get in touch with you at once if there's a problem. Elderly family members may also require a way of letting you know they need help. And clients, customers, coworkers, and bosses want to have easy access. But some of us take our phones—and even laptops—with us on vacation. Answering "emergency" emails from work while sitting on the beach is the most extreme form of multitasking. It defeats the whole idea of getting away from it all, yet people still do it.

Checking email at work, however, is a necessity. The University of Southern California (2019) says that employees typically spend 23% of their day answering emails. They recommend task-switching less often, perhaps allowing yourself to check relevant news for 20 minutes and then switching to email for another block of 20 minutes. Time management hindered by multitasking is a problem for teams as well as individuals. It "creates a higher chance of miscommunication, missed deadlines, and poor work quality." Focusing on one task at a time improves team performance.

5

SELF-CARE AND TIME
MANAGEMENT

W hat does self-care have to do with time management? In part, it depends on how you define self-care. Practicing good self-care can counteract the bad effects of poor time management and wasted time, as well as the anxiety and stress they cause.

WHAT IS SELF-CARE?

Many people think of self-care as an indulgence: a shopping trip, a day at the spa, a bubble-bath, drinks, and dinner with friends. Those may indeed be relaxing, but who has time for them, especially since stress is likely to be with you every day at work? In addition, those kinds of self-care can be expensive. You need self-care that can happen every day, at home or at work, without large outlays of money. Fortunately, that's what true self-care really is.

Self-care is made up of meeting your body's and your mind's basic needs so that you will be able to work better; handle stress better; and not waste time with unnecessary worry about deadlines, schedules, or conflicts. In that way, it helps you achieve better time management. Once you have taken care of your physiological and psychological needs, you'll be better able to manage your workplace performance, including how your time is allotted.

In addition, self-care is a way to remind yourself that you are a person as well as an employee. Incorporating self-care throughout the day is more beneficial than gritting your teeth and struggling through the everyday problems you encounter at work.

Self-care starts at the individual level, and employers can (and should) be proactive in fostering their employees' wellbeing. A good employer will provide information and resources to incorporate self-care into their employees' and their own lifestyle.

YOUR BODY'S NEEDS

Self-care is also known as "workplace wellness." The key word here is "wellness." "Many organizations, including in the private sector, healthcare, and government, have embraced employee wellness programs, seeking to improve staff health, morale and productivity" (Furst, 2019).

Matthew Glowiak (2020) notes, "From a physical health perspective, self-care has been clinically proven to reduce heart disease, stroke and cancer." That means lower insurance costs and less absenteeism, which will be good news for the human resources department; and lighter financial burdens and continued employment—good news for employees.

You already know about the behaviors that can have a long-term negative impact on your health—"eating too much, sleeping too much or too little, or using or overusing alcohol, drugs, and cigarettes" (Furst 2019). But what are the factors that have a positive, healthful influence on wellness at work? Let's take a look at them.

Nutrition

Nutrition is the basis for much of health and wellness. Without the proper nutrients, the body can't function effectively. You can get the vitamins, minerals, protein, and other necessities from multivitamins and supplements available at grocery stores, pharmacies, and health food stores, but eating a balanced diet is even better. Good eating habits can make you feel healthy and full of energy.

Try not to eat lunch at your computer or grab a quick snack from the cafeteria, coffeeshop, or nearby fast-food restaurant. It takes only a few minutes to pack yourself a good lunch. Many workplaces have a break room with a refrigerator where you can keep your lunch fresh.

Don't forget hydration either. Keeping a bottle of water at your desk and substituting it for that third cup of coffee will not only make you less jittery, but also help your system "regulate body temperature, keep joints lubricated, prevent infections, deliver nutrients to cells, and keep organs functioning properly. Being well-hydrated also improves sleep quality, cognition, and mood" (*The importance of hydration*, 2019).

Sleep

Skipping sleep can be a consequence of overscheduling and overwork. It can also be caused by stress, anxiety, and depression. When the difficulties of the day linger and work their way into your home life, your sleep hygiene can suffer. Taking work home and staying up late staring at assorted screens will reduce your ability to get restful, refreshing sleep.

You may realize that sleep not only restores the body, but it influences your mind as well. "Healthy sleep is important for cognitive functioning, mood, [and] mental health... Adequate quantity and quality of sleep also play a role in reducing the risk of accidents and injuries caused by sleepiness and fatigue, including workplace accidents..." (Ramar et al., 2021).

The average human being requires seven to eight hours of sleep for optimal health. It may be tempting to think that you are the exception to this guideline, or you may have heard that important creators, entrepreneurs, and business leaders get by with only four hours or less of sleep a night—but in reality, lack of sleep lowers your ability to work effectively. Don't think that by skimping on sleep you'll have time for "more important" matters. Handling them appropriately will depend on whether you have met your need for sleep.

Physical Activity

Exercise is hard to come by at work. The consequences of sitting at a desk all day, nearly immobile, are profound. They can include weakened muscles, weight gain, and heart disease. When you get home after a tiring day of work, it's hard to find the energy to exercise. But in reality, time spent in exercise will pay off with stress relief, *more* energy, and the stamina to cope with whatever your job throws at you.

When you need a healthy break from work, you could go outside for some fresh air and light exercise. Lunch is the perfect opportunity for you to take a mental and physical break by getting up and going for a walk. Walking around the block can help you clear your mind and refresh your body. Do some light stretching to get your blood flowing. Upper body stretches and isometric exercises can even be performed at your desk.

You spend a lot of time at work. It's important to build an ergonomic workspace that encourages comfort and good posture. Slumping at your computer or tensing up as you type at your keyboard can take its toll on your spine, where many important nerves lie. Pinched nerves or bulging disks can cause great pain and keep you out of work.

Ergonomics is the science of making the task fit the person, rather than the person fitting the task. Some examples of this are allowing workers to sit instead of standing all day, stand instead of sitting all day, or avoid repetitive movements that can bring on carpal tunnel syndrome and other ill effects.

Fortunately, there are many products built with ergonomics in mind that make work life less stressful on your body. With a little research, you can discover ergonomic products that improve your workspace. Ergonomic desk chairs, standing desks, ergonomic keyboards and wrist rests, and other devices are available that will improve your physical health and reduce the amount of time you spend off work from musculoskeletal problems.

YOUR MIND'S NEEDS

Bodily needs are the first things you usually think of when considering health and wellbeing at work. At least as important—or possibly more so—is the condition of your brain and your emotions. How you react psychologically to your work environment has a lot to do not just with your happiness, but with your ability to function in a healthy, productive manner.

Without a proper mindset, any attention to time management is wasted. Being mentally alert and emotionally well-balanced is crucial for making the most of your time at work. If you don't pay attention to these less tangible elements of wellbeing, you will find that your effectiveness at work suffers.

Work/Life Balance

Work/life balance is quite the buzzword these days, and there's a reason for that: It's vital for everyone to achieve in order to get the most out of both areas of life. Time management principles work for both.

For example, to-do lists are ineffective at home as well as at work. We've all had the experience of making to-do lists at home that seem to get longer and longer. Few things are ever crossed off, and the really important things don't get done because of all the focus on minor tasks that eat up time. And multitasking is just as much a myth at home as well. Handling phone calls and emails at home while trying to make or fulfill those to-do lists is impossible, or nearly so.

"We spend roughly a third of our lives at work, so shelving self-care for 'later' just won't cut it anymore" (The Calm Team, n.d.). Many people work on business tasks at home after they leave work. Being instantly accessible is thought to be beneficial to good work and effective time management. Taking work home to finish before bed or after dinner—or instead of dinner—eats up time that could be better spent on self-care.

Especially since the COVID pandemic, companies are increasingly enacting policies that have the effect of helping employees better manage their home and work life. Flextime and telecommuting are two options. Not only can employees work from wherever they are most comfortable, but they can also schedule important self-care tasks such as doctor's appointments and life-enhancing activities like meditation or family outings more easily. Rearranging work time to meet other needs makes for better work life and better home life as well.

Stress Reduction

Self-care, above all, means dealing with stress and anxiety by getting away from them for a while. We've already addressed the topic of stress and anxiety and the bad effects they have on the body and emotions—and therefore on work. But how do you lessen that stress, other than retiring to a desert island? Self-care is one important answer.

Our unique responses to workplace stress must be addressed. "For example, we might notice that stress causes us to feel more anxious, have difficulty concentrating, remembering things and getting our work done" (Mayo Clinic Staff, 2021). If you monitor how you're reacting physically, emotionally, and mentally you can determine when you're under more stress than usual and when it's taking a heavy toll.

Regularly following a daily self-care routine "has been clinically proven to reduce or eliminate anxiety and depression, reduce stress, improve concentration, minimize frustration and anger, increase happiness, improve energy, and more" (Glowiak, 2020). Anxiety, depression, frustration, and anger are negative influences that hinder your work, no matter what kind of career or job you have. Happiness and energy are good for business!

PRIORITIZING SELF-CARE

Self-care alone won't solve all your business problems, but having it recognized as a priority in your job can make a huge difference when it comes to building happier, more sustainable workday routines for you or your employees. Matthew Glowiak (2020) puts it like this: "Although prioritizing self-care may sound like common sense...it's often the first thing to go when we find ourselves in challenging situations." Prioritizing self-care will help you "get away from it all" without going anywhere.

Glowiak adds that the prime "reason people give for not participating in self-care is due to a lack of time. While many of us have a lot going on, it's imperative that we take time out every day for ourselves, even if minimally." Even five minutes of self-care over the course of a day is better than none at all. Cumulatively, it can positively affect your health and wellbeing.

Recognizing that self-care is an important priority in your life has many beneficial effects. Ignoring self-care can add to your stress and make it difficult or impossible to start or maintain healthful habits.

SELF-CARE AT HOME AND WORK

It may seem that self-care is only something to be practiced at home, after work. In reality, it's something that can be done at any time during the day. Self-care activities are not limited to the home life sphere. There are many that can easily be accomplished in either location.

Mindfulness and Meditation

Mindfulness, meditation, and to a lesser extent yoga are sometimes seen in the corporate world as a fix all to the stressors that employees can often feel about their environment and mental health. Nonetheless, they can be important parts of your self-care routine. (People with more severe reactions to anxiety and stress may need professional help.)

Most people have a pretty good idea of what meditation is—a practice in which you try to calm your mind and your thoughts by letting go of what troubles you. Sometimes meditation is done sitting on the floor, but it can also be done sitting on a comfy chair —any place where you are comfortable. The simplest form of meditation is to focus on your breathing, in and out. Counting your breaths is one technique. If you lose count, don't worry, just start again with one. This will help shut off the intrusive thoughts about work and worry that tend to pop into your head throughout the day. You can also focus on an object such as a candle or other sensations such as calming music.

Mindfulness is a lot like meditation, but it involves paying attention to your senses as you go through everyday life and doing tasks intentionally, with attention to what you're doing rather than being distracted by random thoughts or other distractions. Taking a moment to notice what your senses tell you—the touch of your shirt against your skin, the sound of birds outside your window, the sight of a photo on your desk, the scent of flowers you notice on your lunch hour, the taste of the breath mint you just popped into your mouth. This practice grounds you in the real world rather than abstractions like time and busyness.

There are many resources for practicing meditation or mindfulness available on the internet and YouTube. Guided meditations lead you through visualizations and other exercises that will help you relax and focus on something other than work.

Self-care at work is important for combatting feelings of stress or burnout. You can take a moment to do deep breathing exercises or possibly set aside ten minutes on a break for meditation to help yourself feel restored and ready to cope. Meditation at home can be more elaborate—or not. Setting aside even ten minutes for meditating without distractions can go a long way toward shaking off the effects of stress.

Managers can help employees remember to be mindful, fully present, and aware. In addition to preventing feelings of being overwhelmed, it also helps people manage how they view their own and others' emotions and thoughts. When employees see you staying mindful, calm, and centered, especially during stress-inducing situations such as dealing with a customer complaint or finding a clerical error, they're more likely to stay grounded in reality, rather than letting their level of worry skyrocket.

HOW DOES TIME MANAGEMENT FIT IN?

At this point, you may be thinking, all this self-care sounds nice, but how does it help me with time management? Let's look at some ways.

Amy Hanneke (2018) addresses some of the ways time management and self-care mesh: "Blocking your time creates more margin for what matters most, such as time with your loved ones or time resting." Although not typically recognized as a business matter, home life is one of the most important factors in assuring that you and other employees come to work rested, calm, and able to do their best on the job.

Hanneke adds, "Organizing and learning about how you spend time can teach you how to capitalize on your most productive times of day—so there's less time wasted and more time leftover for the end of the day." Portioning your time between work and chores "means that you're less likely to multitask. This can help you feel more closure when turning off your laptop so you can draw more satisfaction from rest."

Basically, managing your time at work enables you to get more out of your home life, and managing your time at home lets you maximize your effectiveness at work. Achieving a balance between the two will make you both more contented and better able to cope with stress. In turn, the lessening of stress will make it easier for you to handle all the surprises that work life holds for you. It's a win-win situation, and self-care can help you achieve it!

6

THE DOMINO EFFECT

Entrepreneur and business guru Gary Keller has a lot to say on the subject of time management in his book *The ONE Thing: The Surprisingly Simple Truth About Extraordinary Results*. The main principle, called "The Domino Effect," helps employers and employees around the world express their vision for their work life and make it into a reality. Let's take a closer look at Keller and his philosophy.

KELLER'S BREAKTHROUGH BOOK

Gary Keller, a Texas-born real estate mogul, burst onto the scene with his first book, *The Millionaire Real Estate Agent,* based on his phenomenal success in that field. Other books followed, until *The ONE Thing,* by Keller and Jay Papasan, was published in 2013. It became a run-away bestseller and Keller was a finalist for *Inc.* magazine's Entrepreneur of the Year. Since then, it has been translated into 26 languages.

Keller has been quoted as saying,

> "If everyone has the same number of hours in the day, why do some people seem to get so much more done than others?... The answer is they make getting to the heart of things the heart of their approach. It's realizing that extraordinary results are directly determined by how narrow you can make your focus" (30 Best Gary Keller Quotes, n.d.).

Keller expands on that idea in his book, saying that prioritizing a single task is the most effective way to accomplish it. Keller calls the priority that is focused on "The ONE Thing"—the big-picture goal—and the steps necessary to reach that goal "The ONE Thing Right Now." One of the main ideas is that spending too much time on too many tasks will result in under-performance. Keller recommends choosing a new "right now" goal every day that will eventually lead to the ONE Thing being accomplished.

Keller notes that, as you work toward your one big goal, your priorities can change and expand. However, he says that "It's always important to keep things in perspective and revisit your top priority" (Ciuca, 2020).

The book also discusses why multitasking doesn't work, how the notion of work/life balance isn't realistic, and that the majority of one's goals will be accomplished the minority of one's efforts (the 80/20 rule). Keller then explains "time-blocking" (which we'll discuss in a later chapter) and how distractions take you away from completing the tasks in your time blocks. Despite this seemingly rigid schedule, the book also stresses the importance of reflection, planning, and relaxation as important to achieving results.

THE ONE THING AND THE DOMINO EFFECT

You may have heard that, in business, bad behavior is like a set of dominos. If one person comes in late every morning and is allowed to get away with it, soon the other employees will think it's okay for them to come in late too. The first person's tardiness has a "domino" or "ripple" effect that leads to bad behavior from many other employees.

Keller's "Domino Effect" is not at all like that, however. His version of the principle refers to lining up your dominos so that they lead to a good effect once the first one is pushed. And that one effect is your ONE Thing, or at least a smaller goal that also leads to it—another domino in the chain, but a larger one.

Keller's philosophy for success involves not just one overarching goal but prioritizing the steps that will take you there. It can be summed up in a simple question: "What's the ONE Thing I can do such that by doing it everything else will be easier or unnecessary?" That's your first domino. "When you line up your dominoes correctly, the collective result of that first, smallest thing is extraordinarily powerful. So when you determine what your first domino is and knock it over, the impact of your action will create a higher level of success" (Ciuca, 2020). After that, you time-block to make sure it happens.

Robert Glazer, Founder and CEO of Acceleration Partners, tells how Keller's philosophy works for him. One year, instead of selecting numerous goals, he picked only four. "Everything else that I would normally set as a goal is now a tactic (domino) to achieve one of my 'ONE thing' goals," he says. "These sub-goals or dominos are the means, not the end" (Glazer, 2019).

Keller's KW Marketing Team (Ciuca, 2020) explains the strategy: Don't try to accomplish too much—you'll get lost in insignificant tasks. They say to give your focus to the single most important thing to accomplish. From there, the Domino Effect will follow.

KEEP YOUR PRIORITY SPECIFIC

There's a temptation to make your ONE Thing too broad. "Become a millionaire" or "be president of the company before I'm 30" aren't specific enough. They may represent dreams you have for yourself, but just try setting intermediate goals for your dominos. You'll end up with things like "Earn $250,000," "Earn $500,000," and "Earn $750,000." Or "Become Department Head by age 22," "Become Vice-President by age 25," "Become Senior Vice-President by age 27." Unless you have specific goals, you won't be able to line up specific dominos to arrive at them.

It's better by far to have a priority you can work toward by realistic increments. "Start my own skin-care business" is much clearer. "Research what products are currently available," "Find a manufacturer who can make small batches of my product," "Start selling online," "Expand the business with new products," "Hire sales staff," and so on are among the possible dominos that might get you started toward your goal.

Your goals can be a little broader than that, though. Keller has said that his priority was that everything he did should be a form of education. That's less specific than "Become a teacher." But starting a consulting business and writing books in his area of expertise are intermediate goals that would fulfill his larger vision —his ONE Thing—and still be doable.

You don't have to be a solo entrepreneur or the head of a corporation to leverage your top priority, either. Keller's Marketing Team has advice for those who find themselves to be ambitious employees—or even ones that just want to succeed within the organization where they are: "Find your ONE Thing, connect it to your company's ONE Thing and become irreplaceable. The employees who attempt to be good at everything but master nothing are ultimately replaceable" (Ciuca, 2020).

Be aware, though, that the dominos can change over time, even if the ONE Thing remains the same. Glazer (2019) explains: "Last year I set a goal to run a half marathon, but I also had an opportunity to bike from London to Paris. Unfortunately, I couldn't do both." This forced him to choose, but, he says, didn't make him feel let down. "Rather than feeling like I did not accomplish a goal, I should have realized both were tactics to reach the same end goal: improved discipline and health."

CHOOSING YOUR LEAD DOMINO

Once you have your priority, or ONE Thing, in place, it's time to consider the dominos. What should be the first one that you push over?

It may be tempting to start with the one that is easiest to accomplish. But consider both which dominos will topple the rest and the thing that will bring the most results. Remember the 80/20 rule—20% of the work will produce 80% of the results. Pushing over the first domino will allow the other dominos to fall, so you should select the most effective.

To continue the situation suggested earlier, creating your own skin care business, the first domino could be "Research the competition." Whom will you be competing against? What are their best-selling products? Is there a gap in their product lineup that you can fill? The next might be "Determine what product you want to sell." Is it a moisturizing cream? A sun-blocker? A concealer? It follows logically from the analysis of the competition—your first domino on the way to your ONE Thing.

The first domino may not be the easiest—it probably won't be —but it can have the largest effect on your plans. You may be tempted to start with an easier domino that you think you can accomplish quickly, such as "Devise a logo and label." That would undoubtedly be more fun and take less time, but it is not the one domino that will put the others in motion.

Knowing what your competition is doing and what product would therefore meet a need in the market are much more important, though they will take a greater investment of time. You can get to the more exciting stuff later. There's no use designing a logo and label for your product if you don't know what that product should be.

In fact, the first domino should probably be the one task that takes the longest and that you most *don't* want to do. Gathering information on the competition and studying that will take considerable effort. And it may be a task you consider dreary and unrewarding. In terms of your dominos, though, it will give a bigger push to the rest. You can get to the smaller stuff afterward. Those details will likely take up more time when considered together, but they're not the 20% that will have the greatest effect. They're small stuff compared to knowing what you should be selling.

The most important domino will change as you move along with your plans, too. At some point, you should prepare a spreadsheet to track your sales and a financial template to record your production costs, overhead expenses, profit, and losses, among other factors. These will be more important and more onerous to do than having business lunches with potential distributors. They will provide more benefit in the long run.

THE DOMINO EFFECT AND PSYCHOLOGY

The domino effect has an exact definition in psychology: "The Domino Effect states that when you make a change to one behavior it will activate a chain reaction and cause a shift in related behaviors as well" (Clear, 2016). In this case, you're making a change to your time management behavior, and the results are increased productivity, less stress, and better performance at work.

Essentially, changing your time management behavior using the domino principle will lead to the first domino falling, creating a cascade of increasing effects. For example, good time management will result in less procrastination, less giving in to distractions, and less temptation to multitask. By lessening your tendency to perform actions that hinder your performance, the domino principle will improve your good habits and negate the bad ones.

"The Domino Effect capitalizes on one of the core principles of human behavior: commitment and consistency" (Clear, 2016). This means that by committing to better time management, you will behave more consistently. Every day that you try new, more effective methods of time management, you will consistently reap the benefits.

Habits form in the brain when you receive a reward for performing a particular action. They are reinforced by the positive outcome, so you are more likely to perform that behavior again. Repetition aids in the process. The brain stores memories by making connections between neurons that get used in doing a certain action. The more the connections get reinforced, the easier ideas are for you to remember. Therefore, the more you repeat the actions, the more likely you are to continue to do them. In terms of time management, you reinforce the areas of your brain that you use for scheduling. In turn, the neural pathways that were created by procrastinating or multitasking will be weakened.

You'll also find that changes you make in one part of life—business—improve not only your work life, but also your personal life. The two are interconnected. Getting your work done more efficiently means that you have more opportunities to engage in other pursuits, such as spending time with family or friends, pursuing hobbies, or finding ways to get rid of anxiety and stress which may have been building up for years. If you try time management and see the results, you will be even more likely to commit to the practice and still see more results.

THE DOMINO EFFECT AND TIME MANAGEMENT

The Domino Effect is at the heart of Keller's time management system. It's necessary, he says, because "it is not that we have too little time to do all the things we need to do, it is that we feel the need to do too many things in the time we have." He has also been known to say, "You can do two things at once, but you can't focus effectively on two things at once. You need to be doing fewer things for more effect instead of doing more things with side effects" (30 Best GARY KELLER Quotes of 34, n.d.).

Specifically, Keller recommends that you be proactive and stop distractions before they start: "Let the people who are most likely to seek you out know when you will be available to them and commit to not leaving your workspace unless it is for bathroom breaks." Here's another Keller tip for managing your time: "If you want to get the most out of your day, do your most important work —your One Thing—early, before your willpower is drawn down… Use it when it's at full strength on what matters most." (Ciuca, 2020).

The immediate goal of the domino principle is to see progress, not overnight results. One week or even a month of managing your time to eliminate bad habits and promote good ones won't automatically get you to your ONE Thing. It will help you make progress toward it. Once you see the dominos begin to fall, you'll realize what a powerful influence this way of thinking has. The progress you make will reinforce your ability to make the domino principle work for you.

For example, a daycare center owner who wants to become an influencer in the field of early childhood education might give a presentation at a conference on how hiring the right people leads to success. Preparing for that presentation involves a certain set of dominos, while giving the presentation itself will be a domino toward her larger goal of becoming a positive force in the industry.

Mindfully focusing on the process—the domino principle—lets you home in on the steps you must take to reach your goal, rather than dwelling on the distance you have to go to reach it. You can even rearrange the order of the dominos as you discover that the path you are on leads to other dominos that need to topple. If the dominos that you set up are no longer taking you toward your goal, you can regroup and consider which ones will.

What does mindfulness have to do with it? When you are mindful, you concentrate on the "now." Neil Farber (2012) explains, "We will do a better job at the task at hand and greatly improve both our chance of success and our satisfaction if we are living fully in the moment." You shouldn't lose sight of your ONE Thing, but you should concentrate on what you can do right now to reach it.

7

HOW TO SCHEDULE YOUR TIME

Now that you've figured out what your number one priority is and what steps that will lead to that outcome, it's time to start scheduling your time. There are some important considerations and several methods of scheduling. We'll take a closer look at the time management tool called "time-blocking" in the next chapter. For now, let's look at what you can do to get yourself ready to make your time work for you, instead of the other way around.

THE HIERARCHY OF TIME

The most common way of scheduling time is to follow these rules.

The first is to look at how much time you have available to spend. Most likely, you will start with a 40-hour week, five days long. This can vary, of course. If you're a lawyer, for example, your boss may require you to work on weekends or more than a 40-hour week. If you have to travel on business, you may have to fly on a Saturday and be able to do some work on the plane. If you're a sole entrepreneur or freelance worker, your hours may change from week to week. Or, if you're bucking for a promotion, you may want to work extra hours to impress the powers-that-be of your dedication. Whatever amount of time you have available is the basis for your schedule.

Next, you think about what actions are essential and what are merely high priority. Your yearly evaluation with your boss, for example, is essential. You have to be there at whatever time they specify. Another essential priority might be checking in with a team you supervise to make sure that they are accountable for their time and efforts. You can even have personal matters as essential priorities, depending on what you value most. In many cases, vacation time may be essential, whether that's a long weekend in a lodge or two weeks on a cruise. That would indicate that you value self-care issues or time with your family.

Then, you triage high-priority activities—ones that are not as urgent as essential priorities. You might find that meetings with the coworkers on your team are an important part of your work life. If you're a sole entrepreneur, your high priorities may be very different. You could prioritize dealing with supply chain issues or a meeting with your biggest client. These are things that you can't easily reschedule.

Next, you schedule time to deal with emergencies. This is harder to do because you don't know when they will pop up. You may find yourself dealing with them after the fact—the emergency arises, but you aren't able to do anything about it because of your essential responsibilities. When you have a big enough emergency, you may have to reschedule some of your high-priority tasks, if you remind yourself to get back to them as soon as possible.

After that, you get to your discretionary or personal time. You will probably schedule this time around your other activities instead of moving other responsibilities to make room for it. Achieving a balance involves weighing your personal time against your normal routine. For example, you may have spending time with your family as a priority in your life. But if one of those emergencies—a machine you use for manufacturing breaks down or your boss is ill, for example—cuts into your personal time, you may have to miss out on your son's class play or bump your getaway weekend to a later time.

Finally, you analyze your time management to see what worked and what didn't. You may find that you have various activities classified in the wrong categories—something that you thought was essential was really only high priority or vice versa, for example. The next time, weekly or monthly, that you have to come up with a plan for your time, you'll do better.

Another thing that may come up while you're considering your priorities and how to schedule them is how other people fit into your schedule. Can you delegate preparing that training on a new computer system to someone on your team who might have some previous IT experience? Would one of your subordinates be able to step in and take over running a team? Another way to shift responsibilities so that you can do your essential tasks is to outsource. Maybe you don't have to do everything yourself. Is there a financial services company in your area or an accounting firm that you can hire to keep track of your expenditures instead of trying to do it yourself?

In the next chapter, we'll discuss a way to systematize your responsibilities and make them run more smoothly. Time-blocking is a more precise and effective method of organizing your tasks.

DEADLINES—START AT THE END

One effective way to schedule your time is to start with the result you want—chairing a meeting or giving a presentation at a business convention, for example—and working your way backward to when you should start every facet of that task.

Let's use those examples. You know when that meeting is to be held and when your speaking slot is at the convention (and the date that the convention will be held). That's the end point that you want to reach and the time when you need to have all your tasks accomplished. You know that the dominos that will lead you to success include researching your topic, making an outline, fleshing out your outline, writing the report you plan to present or the hand-outs that you want to give to participants, and duplicating them.

Making the handouts will not take much time—you estimate 15 minutes. So, if the meeting or presentation is to be at 3 p.m. on Friday, you know that you should have the handouts ready to duplicate by 2:45 p.m. You may want to give yourself a little extra time in case someone is using the printer or copier. Building in time for contingencies like that is a good idea. So, you determine that you need to start copying the handouts at 2:30 p.m.

You estimate that it will take you two hours to write the handouts. That means that you should start writing at 12:30p.m. But wait! You forgot to include time for lunch. Maybe you should begin writing at 9 a.m. You should finish writing by 11 a.m., which gives you plenty of time to write some more if your time estimate was too short or if you decide you need an additional hour to proofread your handouts before you print them.

Then take another step backward in your planning. In order for you to write, you need an outline that is fleshed out. Say you think it will take an hour to write the outline and a half-hour to "fill in the blanks." That means that, working backward, you should start writing at 7:30 in the morning. But perhaps you know you don't do your best work at that hour of the morning, or you have a breakfast meeting to attend. You need to jump back to Thursday and schedule your time for outlining that afternoon. You could schedule outlining and revising for 2 in the afternoon. That means that you will have a finished outline by 3:30 p.m. and can have the rest of the day to spend on smaller, less important tasks.

Next, you need to estimate how long it will take you to research your topic—reading articles on the same or a similar topic, making notes on what you read, watching a YouTube video or TED Talk on the subject, and so forth. You estimate three hours for finding resources and reading or viewing them. You can easily schedule a time block that long in the morning on Thursday between 8:30 a.m. and 11:30 a.m.

If you follow this system, you will know that you should start Thursday morning and work most of the day to have handouts ready for your presentation on Friday afternoon at 3 p.m. If you have other tasks scheduled for Thursday—or worry that you have misjudged the time it will take for each of your tasks—of course, you can spread out your preparation time and begin part of it sometime on Wednesday. Either way, you won't end up on Friday hustling to get done or handing out an inferior product to those attending your presentation.

SCHEDULING SPECIFICS

How much time should you schedule for various types of tasks? That depends on a number of factors. Some tasks come with limits already specified. Your boss may hold a regular one-hour meeting every week and enforce beginning and ending times. That's easy to schedule—it's a given. Or you may have a quarterly sales meeting or a training session that lasts the better part of two days.

But what about other tasks? You can estimate how long they will take, then revise your estimate when you discover how long they really last. Or you can schedule meetings that you control based on how long you want them to last. Alex Iskold (2015) suggests these approximate times: 30 minutes in the office to get to know someone; 45 minutes for a similar in-town meeting outside the office (don't forget to schedule travel time!); 10 minutes for a phone call with a customer who needs advice; and a 30-minute weekly staff meeting.

You may also want to have regular stand-up meetings in a central area of the office. All the participants on a team, perhaps five or six persons, stand in a circle, and each has three minutes to present an update on what they are currently working on or a problem they're having. You can be sure the meeting won't run long—no one likes to stand in one place for more than 15-20 minutes.

You could also book specific times for phone appointments with clients: "I'll call you tomorrow at 2 p.m." or "I can get back to you right after lunch. Are you available then?" Of course, you wouldn't want to do this with your best client, who expects you to be available whenever they call, but for many phone engagements, you can lessen the interruption to your day by dealing with a call a little later rather than immediately. Mention a few possible times for a call-back to accommodate their time needs too.

Review your schedule at the end of the week, say, late on Friday, to determine how well your scheduling efforts worked. Did meetings start and end on time? Did you have trouble scheduling appointments at times that were agreeable to both parties? How much did travel time add to your out-of-the-office meetings? Take what you learned into account when you are planning for the next week.

DAILY AND WEEKLY GOALS

Your time management efforts will run much more smoothly if you consider not just what your goals are, but also how you will know when you have accomplished them. You may have heard people refer to SMART goals—ones that are Specific, Measurable, Attainable, Relevant, and Timely. Naturally, since you're concerned with time management, you might focus on timely goals, such as scheduling your employees' hours two weeks before they actually work. But the other metrics are important as well.

Specific goals are better than ones with a lot of "give" in them. For example, instead of "meet with clients this week," put in your schedule how many clients you will meet with or how much time you will spend on client contact. This would also be a measurable goal, since you can say with certainty at the end of the week that you met with four clients or spent a total of three hours on client contact.

Measurable goals are ones you can put a number, or metric, to. You may have a goal of improving customer relations, but how do you know when you've met that standard? You don't because you can't measure it. A measurable goal is one where you can say *how much* you will do and *by when* you will have it done.

An attainable goal is one that is realistic. In other words, don't promise yourself that you'll do more than you're really capable of. To use the same example, a goal of "meet with all clients this week" may not be attainable. You may have other tasks that will take precedence on certain days. Your biggest client might be out of town for the next two weeks. Ask yourself whether a goal is really attainable before you slot it into your schedule.

STRATEGY AND TACTICS

The use of strategy and tactics is a concept borrowed from the military. Strategy is the overall aim and tactics are the steps used to achieve that end. So, for example, if the strategy is to get soldiers ready for their assignments, the tactics might include sending them to boot camp, providing them with the equipment they will need, and holding training exercises that simulate what they will encounter in the field. You can think of each of these tactics as being a goal, too, and include sub-tactics for each. For example, if you want to send your potential service members to boot camp, you will have to make arrangements for a barracks where they can stay, assign instructors, and give the soldiers an orientation.

Notice that several of the tactics need to be carried out in a certain order, while others can be performed at the same time, most likely by different people. So, for instance, you may want to start assembling the equipment while the soldiers are in boot camp. You will need to assign instructors before boot camp begins, and so on.

How does this relate to time management? The overall goal in this example—the ONE Thing—would be to assemble an effective military force. The strategies are very much like lead dominos for each process, and the tactics are the dominos that lead up to them. You need to pay attention to the strategies first and the tactics second and figure out what order the dominos need to topple in. You may need to assign different personnel to each strategy and still more personnel to the tactics.

In business, this would look like setting up teams to be responsible for the tactics, with a team leader to be responsible for the overall strategy. You might want to introduce a new item to your product line, for instance. You would need team leaders to transmit your vision to each team, and separate teams to perform the actual tasks—with help from the team leaders, of course.

You would need a research and development team to design the product. You would also need a financial team to calculate how much you will need to invest in getting the product ready to go to market, and a marketing team to prepare your sales force for the product introduction. Each team will need to separate their strategy into various tasks and schedule their time accordingly.

8

TIME-BLOCKING AND SETTING BOUNDARIES

Time-blocking is an extremely powerful time management tool that helps most people plot out their days, weeks, and months in a way that makes it easier to fulfill their goals. It's easy to get started, and after using time-blocking for a while, you'll develop a skill that will have a profound impact on your scheduling for both work and home life.

WHAT IS TIME-BLOCKING?

Time-blocking is a way to section your day, week, or month into segments that reflect what tasks you need to do and how long you have to do them. Business coach Robert Carroll (2021) describes time-blocking this way:

Unlike a to-do list, time blocking not only tells you what to do but when to do it. This may sound like a scheduling recipe for disaster. But when you've divided your calendar into time blocks, it keeps you task-focused and limits the ability of others to infringe on your time. What's more, instead of following an ever-expanding to-do list, time blocking lets you start each day with a schedule of specific tasks to complete.

Jayson DeMers (2022) compares time-blocking to creating a time budget, akin to a financial budget. He notes, "People say all the time that time is a resource, but not all techniques leverage that... It forces you to dedicate your attention to concrete intervals and, therefore, helps you prioritize... This also helps in identifying sources of waste." When you look at it this way, wasted time is wasted money—something that is very true when you consider various ways of time management. Time-blocking is a great method of remedying that.

Basically, time-blocking means that you fill up your calendar with blocks of time assigned to separate tasks, based on what needs to be done, when it needs to be done by, and when you work best. For example, you might schedule two hours in the morning for writing a report, then one hour for meeting with your boss or your team. In the afternoon, you might schedule an hour for replying to emails and phone or text messages, then three hours for preparing your yearly budget. Schedule time for your lunch break and other breaks, as well. They're important to getting your other work done in the best possible way.

You can even include personal time in your time blocks. If you want to get in the habit of jogging in the morning before breakfast, put in a time block for it. If devoting time to your family is important to you, set aside a block in the evening for dinner out with your spouse or reading stories to your children. If you have a book club meeting once a month or go to the gym twice a week, put in morning, evening, or weekend blocks for those activities as well.

It's recommended that you use a computer scheduling program such as Google Calendar for doing this rather than a paper calendar, which rapidly becomes no better than a glorified to-do list. Other computer programs, such as a timer, may also help with time-blocking. Use them to analyze how long you actually spend on a task and they'll help you get a realistic view of how much time to block out for that task in the future.

The Benefits of Time-Blocking

Time-blocking is so effective because it works on the idea of "single-tasking" instead of multitasking which, as we've noted, is not really possible or effective. Because of the single-task structure, time-blocking can improve your productivity—by as much as 80% (Carroll, 2021).

It allows you to focus your efforts on a single task and do "deep work" that requires your total focus, such as major projects, while sorting your less-deep tasks into a single time block by "task-batching." To do that, you group all your small, similar tasks into a single time block. For example, checking in with all your team members individually could be grouped together as a block. So could checking various social media or making appointments.

With time-blocking, you'll also better understand how long each sort of task takes you to do. For example, you may have a time block of one hour scheduled for writing up your meeting notes to distribute to your team. If you find that it takes you only half an hour, you'll know to schedule less time for it in the future. Then you can schedule that other half-hour for a different task, a break, or dealing with emails.

Time-blocking also allows you to take advantage of your natural work rhythms, or "productivity cycle" (MacKay, 2019). Each of us has a particular time or times of day when we work best. For many people, that's not when we first get into the office, but later in the morning. You may not do your best work close to quitting time, so it's best not to time-block deep work for those hours. You may even get a spurt of energy after dinner, so you could block time then for tasks that can be done at home or for going back into the office. On the other hand, if you need time to unwind in the evening, you can block off time for relaxation or recreational activities. Your particular patterns may vary, so it's important to learn when you're most focused and effective.

Is Time-Blocking Right for Me?

Time-blocking isn't for everyone. Really, it depends on the nature of your work. If your job requires responding quickly to crises or otherwise reacting in the moment to changing conditions, you may find it difficult or impossible to use time-blocking. In other jobs, interruptions are a routine part of your assignments—customer service, for instance. In cases like these, it really won't be possible to set aside blocks of time to devote to a single task or even a batch of tasks. If your schedule dictates that you can't block off an hour or two for concentrated work, you likely won't be able to time-block.

On the other hand, not having a nine-to-five job doesn't mean you can't time-block. An independent contractor, for example, may have more freedom to choose when during the day they work, but they still can benefit from allotting whatever hours they do work to focus deeply on some tasks and sort others into batches. In fact, a freelancer can gain discipline and avoid procrastination by using time-blocking.

A GUIDE TO TIME-BLOCKING

Time-blocking can build on The ONE Thing that we talked about in the last chapter. As you recall, the principle of The ONE Thing is to determine your most important priority and set up your schedule so that every task you do is a "domino" that will lead you to accomplish that priority. Time-blocking is the perfect system for that.

Perhaps your ONE Thing—your overarching goal or priority—is something that will take months or even years to accomplish. Once you break down that vision into a series of action steps, you can use time-blocking to make sure you accomplish them. You might start by prioritizing what you need to do each month, for example, and block off each month with one of those dominoes. Next, determine what needs to happen every week for that to become a reality. Develop a day-by-day plan to accomplish what you need to do that week. Then, fill in the days in your schedule with blocks of time that you can devote to what's necessary that day to drive you toward your ONE Thing. Essentially, you're determining what is the one most important thing that you need to do each month to reach your goal, then determining the one thing you need to do each week, day, and block of hours.

When it comes down to time-blocking days, you could set aside certain days of the week for a related grouping of tasks. For example, you might set Tuesdays aside for marketing matters and Thursdays for financial planning. Then, you would block time on Tuesday mornings for plans for marketing your latest product and your afternoons for tracking the marketing results you're getting for your existing product or products.

It's good to consider what your most high-priority tasks are and block out time for them first—perhaps two or three hours at a time for the most focused and concentrated. After that, set aside blocks of time for tasks that will likely take an hour and a half or less.

Then, fill up the spaces in between the big blocks with the less important things that still need doing every day to keep your organizational system functioning.

Grouping similar tasks together will reduce the amount of task-switching or multitasking that you do. For example, if you set aside a specific, limited block of time for sending out invoices, you won't be switching back and forth between that and filling out your expense spreadsheet.

Remember to schedule blocks for breaks and personal time, too. You likely won't be able to sustain maximum flow time for more than a few hours at a time. Schedule breaks in between with simpler tasks or self-care activities. Then you can come back to your major task blocks with fresh eyes and mind. "Bookend" time blocks at the beginning and ending of the day. These can signal that you're gearing up for work—gathering the materials you need for an important task, for instance. Or you could make an early evening block for personal obligations or winding down after you've accomplished your major tasks and are ready for a lighter activity such as family time or dinner with a friend.

Learning the Process

If you're new to time-blocking, you may want to start with scheduling your most productive hours—whatever hours in the morning and afternoon you do your best work. Those will be the most important blocks of time for accomplishing your one major goal for the day. Any mandatory activities, such as scheduled weekly meetings or even vacation days, can be blocked in first, before you start considering what will be your major focus for the day or week. Then, once you know what hours are available, you can start filling them in with your time blocks. Once you're more accomplished at time-blocking, you can start filling in whole days at a time, including time for your personal life and daily non-work routine—even when you shower in the morning or have dinner in the evening.

Sticking to these schedules may sound regimented, and in a way, it is. But time-blocking is a method for maximizing those hours and days and what you accomplish in them, while leaving time for unexpected tasks that pop up. So, on Fridays, for instance, you might block off an hour of time before you leave the office for any unfinished tasks or preparations for the next week. In the long run, you'll be both saving time and giving yourself more flexibility. Or you can leave "buffers" of ten or fifteen minutes between the larger blocks so that you have some time to deal with small but urgent matters. When something doesn't fit in easily with your time blocks, you can work it in during these buffers.

And don't forget to block in those break times—above all, you want to avoid burnout! You may even want to set aside a "free" day or half-day to catch up on what you weren't able to fit into your weekly time blocks. You want your schedule to have some flexibility.

Once you've been time-blocking for a while, you can start to create a template that lets you schedule a week or even a month at a time. You could start by allowing yourself larger time blocks for most productive hours but filling in the actual tasks that you'll do during them later. You could set up specific times every day for dealing with organizational "clutter"—email at 1:30 p.m., for example, right after you get back from lunch.

What to Remember

There are certain things that can derail your careful efforts at time-blocking. Keep an eye out for them and avoid them as much as possible.

One problem you may encounter, especially when you first start time-blocking, is underestimating or overestimating the amount of time each task will take. If you underestimate, you'll risk running into later time blocks or not completing your ONE Thing for the day. If you overestimate the length of time to block out, you'll be left with time on your hands. That may sound good for accomplishing smaller tasks, but it can also mean you fall back into the habit of trying to handle too many little things at once and multi-tasking.

It can be a mistake to follow your time blocks too strictly. Say you have a time block for a morning jog, but one of your children gets sick—or you do. Obviously, then, that time block is going to have to yield to the realities of the situation. Similarly, if you have a time block set aside for polishing an ad campaign and approving the graphics for it, but your boss calls a mandatory meeting, you'll have to rearrange your time blocks. Perhaps you can shift your time block to later in the day, to the next day, or to that free catch-up day that you cleverly scheduled for the end of the week.

You should keep your time blocks specific. It doesn't do as much good to block off time for writing when you don't say writing *what*. Your priority—your ONE Thing for the day—should be more specific: writing the analysis of your competition or writing the introduction to your thesis, for example. If you just time-block for writing, you may find yourself switching back and forth between two or more projects and not accomplishing the one that needs doing most, the one that puts you a step closer to your ultimate goal.

Do your best to schedule everything you need to do during a day, week, or month. If you've forgotten one thing, it will suddenly knock all your time blocks off track. Those dominos will start falling in the wrong direction or just scatter randomly, bringing you nowhere close to where you want to be.

Getting an early start on your time-blocked day will help ensure that it runs smoothly. Don't give in to the snooze button! If you need something to get you going in the morning, block time for a hot shower or a visit to a coffee shop to wake you up and get you primed for the rest of the day.

You may not want to schedule a deep work time block for your first block of the day, either, unless that's when your productivity cycle is at its peak. Many people, though, need to ease into the morning with a less laser-focused task. Bookend your most concentrated time blocks with smaller, lighter ones or short breaks so that you don't exhaust yourself by sustaining maximum effort during all your time blocks.

GUARD YOUR TIME BLOCKS WITH BOUNDARIES

What do boundaries have to do with time management and time-blocking?

It's no use time-blocking if no one else recognizes and respects your method of time management. That's why it's necessary to set boundaries. Boundaries are ways of protecting your time blocks so that you can use them to the best advantage. Basically, it requires learning to say "no" and making it stick. Setting boundaries requires good communication skills and a bit of assertiveness to work.

Having boundaries means that you agree to do certain things and specify the things that you won't agree to do. If no one respects your boundaries around time-blocking, your attempt at this form of time management won't do much good. If everyone feels that they can interrupt you at any time, that will disrupt your time blocks and your periods of concentration on the most important thing you need to do.

There are two types of boundaries. The first is a "hard" boundary—something that you will not do, no matter what. For example, you could have a policy that you won't socialize with coworkers outside of work. This could be because you want to keep your family activity time blocks reserved for just that. In that case, you set your boundary and stick to it. Politely but firmly, say no when your team asks you to come for a drink after work with them.

A "soft" or permeable boundary is one that you will alter somewhat under some circumstances. To continue the example, you might have a general policy of not letting work encroach on family time-blocks, but you might make an exception if your spouse has a yoga class that evening, or your kids' soccer game is canceled because of rain. If you do make an exception, you should let your coworkers know that you're not going to make after-work drinks a regular thing, but that you can join them for this particular occasion.

It's best to let everyone know that you will be time-blocking, so that they know when you will be available to them. Explain that some of your time blocks are hard boundaries, when you shouldn't be disturbed at all, while others are more permeable—you could answer brief questions without any difficulty. For longer engagements, you might want to establish a specific time block for working through problems with the team. You can even schedule regular "office hours" when your team knows that you'll be available for meetings and consultations with them. Within those hours, you could conceivably have "appointment slots" during which you'll be available to individuals.

You may be used to saying "yes" to every task that's been assigned to you. However, there are limits to what you can time-block into your schedule. Sometimes, the amount of tasks becomes simply overwhelming. Sometimes, you simply have to stick to your guns and set a boundary by saying "no."

You may well need to practice setting your boundaries. It may be better to say, "I'm sorry. I can't do that project right now. I have a deadline that I can't miss. Maybe Janet can take it on. I'm sure she's capable of it."

And you may have to repeat yourself if one of your coworkers repeatedly ignores your boundaries. Again, be firm but polite: "No, I can't handle this problem right now. Get with me first thing in the morning and we'll work on a solution," if that's when your time blocks have greater flexibility.

Naturally, you can't control all interruptions. Maybe your boss springs a surprise trip to a business convention or an important client meeting on you. Maybe the team you manage encounters a problem that won't wait or a deadline you face is suddenly moved up. You may not be able to set boundaries around such emergencies. You'll just have to adjust your time blocks to accommodate them. If this happens now and then, you can probably adjust your time blocks to compensate. If it happens continually, though, you may need to reexamine whether your job is really suited to time-blocking.

9

WHEN LIFE THROWS YOU CURVEBALLS

L ife never goes exactly as you plan. There are always bumps in the road, whether they are minor inconveniences or absolute catastrophes. Since change is always a part of life, you need to be able to react to it—and you need to do it in a way that furthers your ultimate goals.

That's easier said than done, of course. Paradoxically, it takes planning to be able to shift gears when something unexpected happens to upset your plans. In other words, you need to prepare for the "what ifs" that will inevitably come, even though you don't know exactly what they will be.

STRUCTURE VS. FLEXIBILITY

Time-blocking—indeed, all of time management—is about structure. It involves putting structures in place that will keep you organized, productive, and effective. But those structures shouldn't be too rigid. On occasion, you need to be able to "go with the flow."

Think of your time blocks as potentially flexible. Yes, they're designed to keep you on track—but if life doesn't stay on track, you need to be able to adapt. That's why you build in "catch-up" days or less-busy afternoons for putting out fires or shifting your tasks to a time when you'll be able to take care of them. Remember, the ONE Thing is paramount. Each step that leads to it should be planned, but it doesn't actually have to be done at 3 p.m. or your plan is wrecked.

We've all had to deal with a recent, profound, and unexpected occurrence that changed our lives, both at work and at home—the COVID pandemic. Most businesses, as well as individuals, suffered severe setbacks. The hospitality industry, for example, was devastated. Government mandated shutdowns and masking requirements, supply chain issues, and worker shortages proved too much for some restaurants.

Others survived, through a combination of structure and flexibility. Restaurants that had never done so implemented delivery services to cater to people who were staying home and kept their businesses going that way. Some relied on contingency plans they had in place before the pandemic or made arrangements with their landlords to postpone their rent payments until they were back on their feet again. They applied for government-sponsored emergency business loans. They kept their key employees on, even at reduced wages. The structures they had in place for hiring, supplying, advertising—most aspects of their business—had to be flexible enough to keep their owners' priorities intact.

There were different problems for different businesses. Technology proved a boon to many. Work-from-home options proved beneficial to both employees and companies that invested in computers, networks, and cloud innovations. It surprised many how much of their operations could be kept in place by using their previous means of working but altering how that work was done. Sales meetings and customer contact, for example, were conducted via teleconferencing rather than in-person meetings. Some even learned that their priorities could still be met—and their travel budgets reduced—if they continued these practices even after the pandemic began to ease up.

PREPARATION VS. REACTION

Plenty of possible problems await you. Your power may go out. You could lose your best client. You might even lose your job. While the specific remedies you put in place for those eventualities will differ, your approach should be the same—be prepared.

Some problems you can anticipate, even if you don't know when they'll happen. You know that your computer could crash. They almost always do, sooner or later. It helps if you have made contingency plans ahead of time, so that you won't waste valuable time reacting to the situation.

Have a laptop on hand in case your desktop machine crashes. You may even want to hold onto your old computer; a slow machine is better than no machine. Make sure it's loaded with the same programs you use every day. And you are keeping backups of all your work, aren't you? Learn how to transfer them to that laptop in case of emergency. Locate the nearest reliable computer repair place and have their number programmed into your phone.

Other problems you can't possibly anticipate, so it's next to impossible to plan for them. In those cases, about all you can do is to react to them. But even your reactions can, to some extent, be planned. Having regular fire drills, for example, is a form of preparation for a fire. You may have no idea when or if a fire may strike your building, but if you and your coworkers and employees know where the emergency exits are, you have a much better chance of surviving to work another day. Not being prepared—not having or ignoring fire drills—can cost you much more than a place of business.

Being "proactive" is what we say when we mean "be prepared." It's much better than being "reactive," or responding to crises only after they have already occurred. Proactive strategies are preferable because they minimize the effects of the unexpected, which tend to multiply if they are not prepared for. Reactive actions leave you playing a game of catch-up that can paralyze your business for an unforeseeable period.

RESILIENCE

Planning and preparation will only take you so far, though. Sometimes circumstances change, and there's nothing you can do about it. All you can do is adapt. Resilience is the ability to do just that. It's being able to pivot when necessary—it's the art of bouncing back.

Suppose that you manufacture a product and the cost of one of the raw materials has just increased significantly. The first thing you'll probably want to do is triage—assess the situation and a variety of possible responses to it. The first thing that may occur to you is to raise the price of your product. But is that the only solution?

Perhaps you could find a cheaper source of supply for the raw material. Maybe you could make cuts in other areas of your business to accommodate the increased spending. You might consider toughing it out if you think you can manage until the economy changes, or another source of the material becomes available. The fact is, you have choices, and being able to analyze them is a valuable skill when it comes to dealing with the unexpected.

But you may not know how long the short supply and higher prices will go on. One reaction may not be sufficient. You could need to put in place a short-term plan—paying the higher price— and be prepared to shift to a longer-term strategy—finding a new source—if the problem should continue. Don't be too hasty to put drastic solutions in place, though. If the problem should prove to be less severe than you thought at first, you may have a hard time retreating from your new position.

Remember that you don't have to formulate all the possible responses by yourself. Turn to other people in your organization and ask them for suggestions on how to deal with the crisis. You never know where a good idea is going to come from. Having a corporate culture that values innovation and collegial ways of working, and one that doesn't make people afraid to speak up or take risks, will make it easier to deal with crises with input from everyone.

Above all, put time in your schedule for thought, research, analysis, and planning. If you try to react to something unexpected immediately, you may not come up with a viable solution. Of course, if the problem is really crippling, you may have to put a stop-gap measure in place until you have time to think properly about how to deal with it. It's like using a tourniquet to stop the bleeding while you take the patient to the emergency room, where they can get the treatment, they really need.

KNOW THE FACTS

You may naturally react to the unexpected by catastrophizing—expecting the worst, or even believing the situation is worse than it really is. This doesn't help; indeed, it's counterproductive.

Think about when the brakes on your car go out. You may panic, thinking that it will cost you thousands of dollars and a lot of time to replace the whole system. Instead, it may be only one part, such as the master cylinder, that needs to be replaced. You've added to your own stress by reacting too quickly and not bothering to learn the facts first.

The facts may need updating from time to time as well. During the COVID pandemic, the threat, and the recommendations for fighting it changed from week to week, based on the rate of infection, the availability of vaccines, and other factors. Businesses and entrepreneurs had to pivot based on the latest information from federal, state, and local governments, and health officials such as the doctors of the CDC.

So, think about why that important client left, for instance. The facts will alter how you respond. Did they relocate to another state? Put aside time to prospect for more clients. Consider whether finding two smaller clients might be better than one big client—that way you won't be in such a bind if they leave. But what if they left because of poor service or no follow-up? Then what you need to do is to straighten up whichever department dropped the ball—sales, marketing, customer service, production. It might be time to put in place some retraining.

Concentrate on what happened rather than the money you lost, for example. Do you know why your business took a downturn? The local economy or national trends? Not having the right people or systems in place? Consider it a lesson learned and move on from there. Get back to your main priority as soon as possible—don't give up on it. Just do what needs to be done and go forward from there.

Know what resources you have available or where to find new ones. If your operation takes a severe downturn, your priority becomes recovery. Part of that is staying positive, but another big part is turning to people and organizations around you. Is there a Chamber of Commerce you can join? Are there networking opportunities at the local Junior League or women's business group? You probably should have been proactive and joined these organizations before you experienced a crisis.

Is it time for you to take a class in bookkeeping or marketing at the local community college? Know what's available—or consider online courses. If you need new employees to get your business back up and running, don't just rely on signs or newspaper ads (no one looks for jobs there anymore). Check out local temp agencies. Lots of their clients are dying for a temp-to-permanent position.

FOCUS ON SOLUTIONS

When a crisis hits, it's perfectly natural to feel a moment of panic. In fact, it may actually be important to do so. You don't want to blow off an eventuality that really will have a significant effect on your plans. But it doesn't help to imagine a worst-case scenario either. What you need to do is acknowledge that a problem has arisen and that you can't ignore it. Once you dismiss both the imagined worst case and the tendency to brush off a problem, then you can get on to the real business of finding solutions.

One of the first things you should do is to consider your assets —and not just your financial ones. It's easy to say that you can fix any problem by throwing money at it, but that's just not true. Almost certainly, while money may be part of the solution, it likely won't solve the whole problem.

People are one of your greatest assets. There are bound to be people within your organization that can help you brainstorm possible solutions. This could be your board of directors, but it could also be someone below you in the organizational chart. People "on the ground" who are involved with everyday tasks may be closer to the solutions because they are intimately aware of how your business functions on the most practical possible level. An apartment complex manager, for example, may have a better handle on what or who could pick up the slack when the snow removal company you relied on goes under. That's not something that a person in the corner office of the property investment company might know.

Asking questions is also important. Taking a step back can be, too. Instead of asking, "How can I solve this problem?" you might do better to ask how you would advise someone else to solve the same problem if they encountered it. It would give you a new perspective on the problem and engage your brain in a different way. Then follow up with the ideas you generate.

Once you have a solution in hand, though, don't shut down the source of ideas. For one thing, the situation may change again, requiring you to pivot once more. For another, you can keep solutions you didn't try this time in the back of your mind. They may be the answer to the next crisis that comes along or show you a way you can prepare for it.

FOCUS ON PRIORITIES

It's easy to get bogged down in problems when they arise, or to lose focus. But your primary aim should still be paramount. If your goal is to publish a book, for example, but you aren't able to finish writing it because of a family crisis, keep your goal in mind. You may not be able to get back to work on it for a while, but as soon as you are able, get back to it. Don't abandon your project and take up a different one, like opening a business instead. Or, if you discover that your book isn't turning out like you wanted it to, don't lose your goal of publishing a book—take a different idea for a book and run with that.

The steps you set in place—the dominos that you need to get the momentum started and keep it going—can remain the same. You'll still be able to time-block for writing, for researching the competition, and for planning your marketing strategy for the new book.

Focusing on your priorities will help you ward off potential negativity. It's only natural to feel somewhat down after a setback. But you can't allow yourself to wallow in it. When you experience difficulties, you have a chance to learn something from them, which can help you get back to your old success.

TAKE A BREAK IF YOU NEED TO

You may have experienced a setback but working twice as hard may not get you out of that hole. You may end up frantic, scrambling, working unsustainable hours until you can't work anymore. That's not a way to realistically cope. It only leads to burnout—and maybe an enforced break when your health suffers.

Remember what we said about self-care? Is the stress getting to you? Are you having migraines? Trouble sleeping? Some people would tell you that's the time to redouble your efforts. But is it really?

Instead of redoubling, maybe it's time for you to regroup. Taking a break to recover your health and your spirit doesn't mean you're giving up. It means you're going to go back to work better than ever.

How much time off is enough and how much is too much? That depends on the circumstances. Maybe you just need to take Friday afternoon off and not push yourself to do work on the weekend if your problem is modest. A day or two can help you unwind and allow you to return with renewed energy to solve your problems.

If you've experienced a profound loss, however, such as the death of a loved one, you should take off all the time you need to. No one can tell you how long grief should last. When you come back, you will work better than you would if you had forced yourself to return to work before you were really ready to devote yourself to your tasks. That's part of self-care.

To be ready for such an occasion, make sure beforehand that there is someone who can take over your duties until you return. Tell your assistant or second-in-command where your time-blocked calendar is and how to access it—do this before the need arises. Make sure they understand the concept of time-blocking so they can take over in your absence. It's better to be proactive rather than reactive.

YOUR TIME MANAGEMENT PLANNING GUIDE

Much of this guide has assumed that you will be doing most of your time management on a daily, weekly, or monthly basis. What about longer-term planning? Is that advisable or even possible? Let's take a look at how you can plan for the long term.

HOW FAR AHEAD IS TOO FAR ?

Daily, weekly, and monthly time-blocking may be the norm, but there are other lengths of time that should be considered. Among them are quarterly and half-year planning. Planning a year at a time or longer is more problematic. While it can help with seeing whether you reached your expectations and met your metrics or goals, time-blocking for a whole year is not really feasible. Too many things can happen that would cause you to pivot or revise your plans.

Quarterly planning is pretty common in the business world, and even in education. A lot of companies set quarterly goals for production or sales, for example. These goals provide a means of holding employees accountable. They can even help promote weekly or monthly time management. If a member of the sales-force knows that they are expected to bring in $300,000 per quarter, they will realize that in order to meet that goal, they will have to bring in $100,000 per month and can plan accordingly. Six-month goals and yearly goals can similarly be used to track progress, provide accountability, and aid in planning.

Much farther ahead than that is less likely to be helpful. You can have a goal of running a $5,000,000 company within two years but breaking that down into yearly or monthly increments is not likely to be possible. There are too many unknown factors that will play a part in what happens. You may encounter any number of crises that will impede your progress. A long strike by employees can disrupt your business and is impossible to plan for because you don't know how long it will last. A downturn in the economy or a rise in inflation may cause your stock to go down. Stagnation in research and development may not be due to any deficiencies in the staff but can be caused by reaching the limits of one avenue of investigation.

How you respond to such situations will determine whether your yearly goals—or longer ones—are feasible or not. In these cases, flexibility in your responses will be more likely to result in meeting your goals.

Scaling back, reducing the workforce, or moving to a less expensive location might be necessary. And your goals may have to change. Your overall priority—your ONE Thing—can remain the same, but how you reach it will have to change with the circumstances. And this will disrupt your time management. All the daily, weekly, and monthly plans you made will have to be altered. For example, if you have an overall priority of becoming the leader in your field, but you have to downsize, you will naturally have to change the dominos that lead to your goal.

Given all that, it's a good idea to revisit your plans at least quarterly to see how well they're holding up.

REVISIT YOUR SCHEDULE

It may surprise you to know that May is officially Revise Your Work Schedule Month. But whatever month you choose to do it, revisiting and revising your schedule regularly is a great idea.

You may not want to revisit it monthly, though. Yearly is better, and quarterly is probably best. Revising your schedule monthly doesn't allow much time for the schedule to "settle in," especially if you are trying time-blocking for the first time. Certainly, you should keep an eye on your schedule and adjust your time blocks, lengthening or shortening ones that you find don't work out as they should. But a total overhaul should wait until you have some more data to work with.

Revising your time blocks quarterly will give you a chance to focus on your dominos. Are they set up in the right order to topple? Can you determine whether there are more or different ones you need to focus on during the next quarter? Revisiting your schedule yearly provides you with the opportunity to look more closely at your overall goal—your ONE Thing. Think of the yearly review as a chance to look at your strategy and the quarterly review as a time for looking at your tactics.

You want to be able to analyze how well your schedule is working, of course, but for that you need metrics. How will you know whether your schedule is working and whether you have been accomplishing what you set out to? During your quarterly review, try to put some numbers to your progress. How much more did you get done with the new schedule during the first month? Was there a measurable increase in your productivity? How much time were you able to spend on self-care and your non-work obligations? Extend that analysis to the other two months as well.

Compare your answers to the goals you had set for yourself. Is your time-blocked schedule working? What might you change that would improve your metrics? Implement those strategies for the next quarter.

Share Your Progress

Naturally, you will want to share your results with your team leader, supervisor, or manager to let them see how your new form of time management is working. Use the analysis of your metrics that you have just conducted to demonstrate concretely the progress you've made. Elicit their suggestions for new goals or dominos you could set up.

You can also use the revision opportunity to encourage any coworkers or subordinates to try time-blocking as well. You will be able to demonstrate to them what you have accomplished and how you have done that. Help them develop time-blocked schedules themselves. Challenge them to discover how their own results can improve the way yours did. If your whole team or division gets on board, you'll have even better metrics to show for the next quarter.

New Ways of Working

While you're revisiting your schedule, think about the new ways of working that have grown up as a result of the COVID pandemic. Working from home and hybrid work are the primary ones, but job sharing, and flex time can also be considered.

Work-from-home plans have multiple benefits. Think about how much time you could save by not having to commute to work every morning. You could use that time to start work earlier—or you could use it to add a morning jog into your routine. You could knock off for an hour in the afternoon to pick up your kids from school or daycare. Best of all, you could schedule your work for the times of day when you're most productive. You'd have more control over what hours you work and what you get done during them. You're more responsible for your own time, so you can make the most of it!

If your job requires you to be on-site at least part of the day, investigate whether you could create a hybrid schedule—working part of the day at home and part of the day in the office. You could use your office time for important meetings and teamwork, then spend your most productive hours at home, where you're less likely to be interrupted. You can send your bosses weekly updates showing how much you've accomplished, so they'll get behind the new way of working and managing your time.

Job sharing can be combined with hybrid working. When you job-share, you complete half the work, and another person then takes over and does the other half. This may make your supervisor more comfortable with letting you work from home. And if you have dreams of building your own business, you can work on that at home while the other person takes over your regular duties.

Flextime also meshes well with time-blocking. With flextime, you don't work regular nine-to-five hours. Instead, you have the ability to fix your own hours, depending on when and how you work best. If you're an early bird, you might want to schedule your time starting at 7 a.m., then two hours off in the late morning or early afternoon when your natural energy is lower. Or you could go to work starting at nine, but work until 6:30 p.m. instead of 5 p.m. As long as you get your work done, does it really matter which hours you do it in?

MAKE YOUR PLANS REALISTIC

You will be less likely to fall into the trap of planning too far ahead if you keep your dreams alive but anchored in the realm of possibility. If your plans are too far-fetched, not achieving them can leave you in despair and possibly even make you feel that you have to give up your dream.

Realistic plans leverage time management. Good time management keeps you from being bogged down by details, but at the same time it allows you to decide which details are really necessary for achieving your goals. You can then treat them as dominos leading to your priorities. For example, writing a sales brochure is a realistic time block that helps lead to your medium-term goal of increasing sales. Planning a beach vacation with your family is an essential detail if your priority is taking care of your mental and emotional health or spending time with your family. Note that the sales brochure could possibly be delegated to someone else, while planning for the trip is something you will want to do yourself—or "delegate" to your spouse or the family as a whole.

Your plans aren't realistic if they are too much for you to achieve in the time you have. For example, hiring and training new personnel is something that you can't accomplish in a week. You'd be much better off scheduling a week or two for collecting resumes, a week for doing interviews with the candidates, and at least two weeks or even a month for your new hires to learn the ropes and become effective members of the team. In fact, you may want to schedule a probationary period of 90 days for them and a performance review at the end of it. These steps can make your business plan into a reality.

Making a realistic business plan is especially important if your priority is starting a new business from scratch. You will definitely need one if you want to attract investors or acquire seed money. You shouldn't fill it with dreams and wishes, but with strategy and tactics and a blueprint on how you will proceed. Be objective and gather the facts. How much competition is there? How will your product or service fill a niche? Be prepared to articulate your vision in terms of executive responsibilities, personnel requirements, marketing plans, and financing proposals. Then you can schedule time blocks for developing each subtopic that underlies your plan —time for researching the competition, time for exploring what kinds of people and resources you will need, time for putting together a prospectus for potential sources of financing.

You may want to develop an "elevator pitch" too—a sentence or two that encapsulates your ideas and catches the attention of the person you're going to propose your plan to. Of course, that's not the entirety of your planning, but it's a good first step to take once you have your complete business plan in place. And you really should include in your business plan a summary of the risks or obstacles that your new business faces. It will not be seen as realistic without that.

THE COSTS OF NOT MANAGING TIME

Exactly how much time are you actually wasting because you don't manage your time well? And how much money do you waste by filling your days with distractions and tasks that are either unnecessary or could be done more effectively by someone else?

There's a way to figure it out. Start by keeping a time log—a record of how you spend a typical day or week. Be sure to include interruptions you encounter, and time spent doing simple tasks like answering emails or text messages.

Next, calculate what your time is worth. Start with your base salary. Divide by 52 to determine how much money you eat up in a week's time. For example, if you make $140,000 a year, every week you work is worth around $2,700 and, given a five-day work week, every day you work is worth a bit more than $500. For an eight-hour day, that makes $60+ an hour.

Then, compare your distractions on the time log to your time-worth per day. If you spend two hours per day on social media time, interruptions, emergencies, busy work, procrastination, and tasks that you could have delegated to someone else, you've wasted $120 of your day's worth. In one week, you'll have wasted $600—more than an entire day's worth. And for the year, you've wasted over $30,000 of your own money—not to mention much more than that of the company's valuable time.

Not managing your time also takes a physical and emotional cost on your body in stress, anxiety, overwork, and potential burnout. This toll is significant, as it can lead to doing not only less work but doing it less well. It can also lead to being forced to work less when your body gives in to a stress-related illness such as heart disease.

When you think of the financial and physical costs of not implementing good time management, you can see that the effort you spend putting it in place will pay off in any number of ways. That's an advantage you want to give yourself both for your own health and the health of your business, education, and personal life as well!

CONCLUSION: LIFE WITH GOOD TIME MANAGEMENT

What will your life look like once you have implemented time management skills? Your work life will be more productive and effective. Your home life will be easier to manage as well. Your physical and emotional health will improve. And you'll be much closer to attaining your overall goals—your ONE Thing priorities.

Let's review the specifics of time management that have been covered in this book.

First, we looked at what *doesn't* work and what keeps you from managing your time well. The typical advice for time management —multitasking and to-do lists—is not really effective.

Multitasking doesn't really exist. What we call multitasking is really task-switching, which uses up brain power and time whenever you try to do it. These small increments of time add up, and the distractions caused by task-switching eat up even more of your valuable time.

To-do lists are difficult to control. They tend to be messy—not prioritized—and include tasks of different kinds in a random order. The time each task on the list will require is not even considered. A list can easily contain tasks that bear a different weight, urgency, or importance. Finding the most important task to do amidst the clutter of multiple tasks is difficult.

There is also a tendency when considering a to-do list to take on the easiest and most pleasant tasks first, which may not be the most important things for you to do. In fact, the task that you least want to do is likely the most important one, the one that will get you the farthest on your path toward your goal.

Another pitfall with to-do lists is overscheduling. To-do lists can quickly grow to lengths that are impossible to accomplish in a day or even a week. You'll end up juggling projects, not spending enough time on any of them to make real progress.

Then there are habits of mind and psychological roadblocks to managing time effectively. These include procrastination, over-thinking, anxiety, and perfectionism. When you procrastinate, you are probably letting the most important tasks fall by the wayside. Putting them off till the next day or the next week will make it harder to come up with a workable schedule for that time period.

You can also overthink your schedule. While some business leaders claim to schedule their time down to the minute, that's not a good option for most executives and employees. With such a tight schedule, any monkey wrench in the works will throw the whole thing off. And estimating how long tasks will take needs some leeway. Do you know in advance if cleaning up your database will take one hour or two? Will multiple meetings take up two hours of your time or half the day? As you get used to time management, you'll be better able to estimate how much time you'll need for one task, but that's all it will be—an estimate.

What's known as "writer's block" happens to other people besides writers. It is an inability to get started on what you know you have to do. No ideas come to you. You give in easily to distractions. Before you know it, you've frittered away time that should have been spent on making progress.

Anxiety will also eat into your time and make it more difficult for you to accomplish anything. Being worried all the time about whether you are using your time effectively will result in just what you feared. And anxiety will take a physical, mental, and emotional toll on you. It is one of the major contributors to burnout, along with stress.

Perfectionism is another stumbling block, much like overthinking. Believing that your work must be perfect down to the smallest detail gets in the way of getting it done. Perfection is really unattainable. There will always be just one more tweak you could make, one more thing you could add, one more person who should be consulted. You can't anticipate every eventuality. At some point, you will just need to say, "good enough" and get on with something else. The world won't stop turning if there's one minor flaw in your project.

What will help make your planning and scheduling more efficient and effective is the 80/20 rule. This says that 20% of your effort will produce 80% of your results. When you give in to perfectionism, you are expending more of your effort than you really need to. The time you invest will shift away from the 20% that will achieve the most and best results. It will become an increasingly large proportion and therefore less effective. The closer you get to spending 80% of your time on one task, the further you get away from the powerful results you could have by actually expending less effort.

Self-care also relates to time management in a number of ways. First and foremost, it can help you alleviate the stress and anxiety that occur when you don't have good time management. This can prevent mental, physical, and emotional effects that will keep you from sticking to your time management plans. Without self-care, your body and mind don't function properly, and your work suffers.

So what does work for good time management? The first thing you need to do is establish your number one priority—your

ONE Thing, according to Gary Keller's philosophy of time management. Then, determine the steps that will lead you to that goal. All the steps in your process flow from—or rather to—that ONE Thing. If you sequence the steps properly, they will be like a line of dominos that you follow to reach your overall vision.

Your time management will work better if you think about your deadlines and work backward from them to determine when you ought to start a project and how much work you need to do each day. It also helps to "triage" your tasks and sort them into categories—essential, high priority, lower priority, and discretionary. You should also consider whether there are other people who could perform one of the lower priority or discretionary tasks and delegate those to them.

The most powerful time management tool of all is time-blocking. When you time-block, you set aside specific lengths of time for your most important priorities. Your lesser priorities can be scheduled next, during the remaining time. You can even put aside some time for performing nonessential, quick-to-accomplish tasks by task-batching—putting like activities together and completing them in a single time block.

Once you have set up your time blocks, you will want to establish boundaries around them. Let the other people in your business know that you are time-blocking and aren't available for distractions during certain hours when you must focus on your highest priority tasks. Learn to say no to requests that take you away from this work. You might even have to create a separate time block for keeping coworkers or team members in the loop.

Finally, realize that unexpected events will happen and that you may need to step in and deal with them right away. If possible, you can prepare proactively to cope with potential emergencies rather than waiting for them to strike and reacting instead. You may want to schedule a "catch-up" day when you will clear up the aftermath of a problem that made you shift your time blocks in order to deal with them.

Remember the examples of Carl, Leslie, and Daniel from the first chapter? Each of them had certain time management problems that left them open to bad results. Using the time management techniques detailed in this book could have helped them all.

Carl wasn't able to present his report because his subordinates didn't give him what he needed on time. He experienced a disruption in his schedule when one of them was ill. And he missed important family and business events when he was reacting to his problems.

Carl could have used scheduling backward from his deadline to make sure he had allotted enough time to prepare his report. He could have shown his subordinates how to time-block so that they would get the facts and figures he needed to him in time. He should have also anticipated that a worker might become ill and had a backup plan in place to shift responsibilities to a coworker. Carl might also have set up time blocks and prioritized spending time for company functions and family and guarding them with boundaries.

Leslie was the microbiology grad student who didn't perform her job well because she spent time consoling a friend, overslept, was late for class, and missed lunch, which made her weak and shaky. She worried that she would lose her job.

Leslie could have benefited from time-blocking and practicing self-care. She should have set aside time blocks for sleep and lunch, which would have meant that she made it to the lab in plenty of time. She should have limited the time she spent consoling her friend by setting a boundary around her sleep time. With an appropriate amount of sleep, she likely wouldn't have been late to class, which should have been another one of her time blocks. And instead of catastrophizing about losing her job and adding to her stress, she should have used all the above methods to make sure she did her job in a timely fashion so that her good performance would mean that she wouldn't have the additional stress.

Daniel was the addiction counselor who worked late every night, leading to difficulties with his husband. He could have blocked time for doing his case reports and showed it to his boss to prove that he was doing all the case reports he could within the eight hours required by his job. He could have made finishing his work on time his priority and said no to requests that impinged on his time boundary. He could also have focused on self-care, both for his own sake and for his husband's.

Good time management could have helped all these people, and it can help you too! Try it yourself—determine what your ONE Thing is and then time-block a week's worth of segments that will lead to you getting at least one domino to topple. Make sure you allow time blocks for task-batching, breaks, and even your home life. Assess what your week was like before time-blocking and how you did on a time-blocked week. Were you able to stick to the time blocks? Did you find that any of the tasks took a longer or shorter time than you had planned for? What would you do differently if you were to extend your time-blocking into the next week? What boundaries could you put in place to "defend" your time blocks? What could you do to be proactive regarding unexpected events?

Once you have the answers to those questions, think about how time-blocking would work for a month at a time. Can you set yourself one or maybe two dominos to build in that would help you work toward your goal? If you can, you're well on the way to good time management.

If you stick to these principles, you can make time management work for you. Along the way, you'll find that you will accomplish more and more effectively, reduce the debilitating effects of anxiety and stress, and improve your life outside of work as well.

There's no reason not to put proper time management in place!

ABOUT THE AUTHOR

Morton Hewitt has spent his career between the corporate world and co-founding businesses. This is Morton's first book, which is the culmination of his life of learned experiences and the lessons and wisdom of his mentors and partners.

A husband of long standing, father of adult children, and a dog lover to the core, Morton grew up in a rural environment, where family and community were at the center of his universe.

Morton has reached that point in life where he feels that to truly show gratitude for life's blessings, he needs to pay forward the knowledge that he has gained over a lifetime.

REFERENCES

Barratt, B. (2019, January 22). How to get out of the bad habit of multitasking. *Forbes*. https://www.forbes.com/sites/biancabarratt/2019/01/22/how-to-get-out-of-the-bad-habit-of-multitasking/?sh=7d60e0776522

Birt, J. (2022, March 28). *14 ways to practice self-care at work (and why it matters)*. Indeed Career Guide. https://www.indeed.com/career-advice/career-development/selfcare-at-work#:~:text=Practicing%20self%2Dcare%20at%20work

Bregman, P. (2020, August 11). Your to-do list is, in fact, too long. *Harvard Business Review*. https://hbr.org/2020/08/your-to-do-list-is-in-fact-too-long

The Calm Team. (n.d.). *Creating a culture of self-care in the workplace*. Business.calm.com. https://business.calm.com/resources/blog/creating-a-culture-of-self-care-in-the-workplace

Carroll, R. (2021, June 22). *Ultimate guide to time blocking: tips and techniques*. BetterUp. https://www.betterup.com/blog/time-blocking

Ciuca, A. (2020, July 9). A quick formula for unlocking your potential: The domino effect. *KW Outfront Magazine*. https://outfront.kw.com/training/quick-formula-for-unlocking-your-potential-the-domino-effect/

Clear, J. (2016, July 19). *The domino effect: How to create a chain reaction of good habits*. James Clear. https://jamesclear.com/domino-effect#:~:text=What%20is%20the%20Domino%20Effect

Coupland, M. (2019, August 26). *The dangers of multitasking and how to stop*. The Ascellus Group. https://ascellus.com/how-cbt-can-help-with-multitasking/

DeMers, J. (2020, July 22). *How to use time blocking for productivity: 19 practical ways*. Lifehack. https://www.lifehack.org/881771/time-blocking

Dorvil, C. (2016, July 1). Council post: How to improve your response to the unexpected. *Forbes.* https://www.forbes.com/sites/theyec/2016/07/01/how-to-improve-your-response-to-the-unexpected/?sh=36efd3204691

Evans, B. (n.d.). *To-do list anxiety: How to overcome it & get things done.* Friday.app. https://friday.app/p/to-do-list-anxiety

Farber, N. (2012, February 7). The domino effect. *Psychology Today.* https://www.psychologytoday.com/us/blog/the-blame-game/201202/the-domino-effect

Fike, D. (2014, May 6). *Planning for the unexpected.* Possibility Change. https://possibilitychange.com/planning-for-the-unexpected/

Gary W. Keller. (2022, October 15). Wikipedia. https://en.wikipedia.org/wiki/Gary_W._Keller

Glazer, R. (2019, January 10). *Achieving goals using the domino-effect.* Robert Glazer. https://robertglazer.com/friday-forward/domino-effect/

Glowiak, M. G. (2020, April 14). *What is self-care and why is it important for you?* Southern New Hampshire University. https://www.snhu.edu/about-us/news room/health/what-is-self-care#:~:text=Engaging%20in%20a%20self%2Dcare

Gray, P. (2021, June 9). *Responding to the unexpected: How you react can make or break your business.* TechRepublic. https://www.techrepublic.com/article/responding-to-the-unexpected-how-you-react-can-make-or-break-your-business/

Grensing-Pophal, L. (2020, March 16). *Best practices for multitasking.* HR Daily Advisor. https://hrdailyadvisor.blr.com/2020/03/16/best-practices-for-multitasking/

Grucela, A. (2022, August 9). *45+ burnout statistics, trends, and facts [2022].* Passport Photo Online. https://passport-photo.online/blog/burnout-statistics/

Haden, J. (2018, July 20). How to write the perfect business plan: A comprehensive guide. *Inc.* https://www.inc.com/jeff-haden/how-to-write-perfect-business-plan-a-comprehensive-guide.html

Hall, J. (2020, January 5). Self-care isn't just good for you—It's also good for your productivity. *Forbes.* https://www.forbes.com/sites/johnhall/2020/01/05/self-care-isnt-just-good-for-you-its-also-good-for-your-productivity/?sh=c20158a19ff3

Hamilton, J. (2008, October 16). *Multitasking in the car: Just like drunken driving.* NPR.org. https://www.npr.org/2008/10/16/95702512/multitasking-in-the-car-just-like-drunken-driving

Hanneke, A. (2018, June 4). *Why time management can be a form of self-care.* Well-Seek. https://wellseek.co/2018/06/04/why-time-management-can-be-a-form-of-self-care/

Ho, L. (2005, December 6). *Why do I procrastinate? 5 root causes and how to tackle them.* Lifehack. https://www.lifehack.org/articles/lifehack/6-reasons-on-why-are-you-procrastinating.html

How to boost your effectiveness by 400 percent. (2021, February 4). *Inc. Magazine.* https://brianpmoran.com/blog-post/how-to-boost-your-effectiveness-by-400-percent/

The importance of hydration. (2017, September 28). Harvard School of Public Health News. https://www.hsph.harvard.edu/news/hsph-in-the-news/the-importance-of-hydration/#:~:text=Drinking%20enough%20water%20each%20day

Iskold, A. (2015, March 29). 7 Tips for managing your schedule like a pro. *Entrepreneur.* https://www.entrepreneur.com/living/7-tips-for-managing-your-schedule-like-a-pro/243962

Jones, M. B. (2015, August 26). *Productivity tip: finding the lead domino.* Climb.pcc.edu. https://climb.pcc.edu/blog/productivity-tip-finding-the-lead-domino

Kim, S. (2021, May 5). Forget to-do lists. You really need a "got done" list. *Wired.* https://www.wired.com/story/productivity-got-done-list/

Laoyan, S. (2022, June 19). *Understanding the pareto principle (the 80/20 rule).* Asana. https://asana.com/resources/pareto-principle-80-20-rule

MacKay, J. (2019, July 9). *Time blocking 101: A step-by-step guide to mastering your daily schedule*. RescueTime Blog. https://blog.rescuetime.com/time-blocking-101/

Madell, R. (2016, October 12). *Planning for the unexpected during your workweek*. FlexJobs Job Search Tips and Blog. https://www.flexjobs.com/blog/post/planning-for-the-unexpected-during-workweek/

Madore, K. P., & Wagner, A. D. (2019). Multicosts of multitasking. *Cerebrum: The Dana Forum on Brain Science, 2019*. https://www.ncbi.nlm.nih.gov/pmc/articles/PMC7075496/

Markovitz, D. (2012, January 24). To-do lists don't work. *Harvard Business Review*. https://hbr.org/2012/01/to-do-lists-dont-work

Martins, J. (2021, May 6). *6 tips to achieve flow state at work*. Asana. https://asana.com/resources/flow-state-work

Mautz, S. (2017, May 11). Psychology and neuroscience blow-up the myth of effective multitasking. *Inc.com*. https://www.inc.com/scott-mautz/psychology-and-neuroscience-blow-up-the-myth-of-effective-multitasking.html

Mayo Clinic Staff. (2021, March 24). *Stress management*. Mayo Clinic. https://www.mayoclinic.org/healthy-lifestyle/stress-management/in-depth/stress-symptoms/art-20050987

Mind Tools Content Team. (2009). *Effective scheduling: Planning to make the best use of your time*. Mindtools.com. https://www.mindtools.com/pages/article/newHTE_07.htm

Minot, D. (2019, July 1). *Self-care is essential to well-being at work*. Behavioral Health News. https://www.behavioralhealthnews.org/self-care-is-essential-to-well-being-at-work/

Multitasking skills: Definition and examples. (2022, October 19). Indeed Career Guide. https://www.indeed.com/career-advice/career-development/multi-tasking-skills

Multitasking: Switching costs. (2022). Apa.org. https://www.apa.org/topics/ research/multitasking

The myth of multitasking. (2013, May 10). NPR.org. https://www.npr.org/2013/ 05/10/182861382/the-myth-of-multitasking

Parker-Pope, T. (2008, November 19). *Multitasking in the car.* Well. https:// archive.nytimes.com/well.blogs.nytimes.com/2008/11/19/multitasking-in-the- car/

Ramar, K., Malhotra, R. K., Carden, K. A., Martin, J. L., Abbasi-Feinberg, F., Aurora, R. N., Kapur, V. K., Olson, E. J., Rosen, C. L., Rowley, J. A., Shelgikar, A. V., & Trotti, L. M. (2021). Sleep is essential to health: an American Academy of Sleep Medicine position statement. *Journal of Clinical Sleep Medicine, 17*(10). https://doi.org/10.5664/jcsm.9476

Rampton, J. (2019, September 12). *The 11 biggest symptoms of poor time manage- ment.* Calendar. https://www.calendar.com/blog/the-11-biggest-symptoms-of- poor-time-management/

Rampton, J. (2020, January 28). How time management can help you avoid burnout. *Entrepreneur.* https://www.entrepreneur.com/living/how-time-manage ment-can-help-you-avoid-burnout/345091

Ritchie, D. (2019, November 12). *Anxiety's impact on time management.* Calendar. https://www.calendar.com/blog/anxietys-impact-on-time-management/

Samuel, A. (2018, March 13). *7 alternatives to a to-do list for people who hate to-do lists.* EAB. https://eab.com/insights/daily-briefing/workplace/7-alternatives-to- a-to-do-list-for-people-who-hate-to-do-lists/

Schawbel, D. (2013, May 23). Gary Keller: How to find your one thing. *Forbes.* https://www.forbes.com/sites/danschawbel/2013/05/23/gary-keller-how-to- find-your-one-thing/?sh=62c8b8307292

7 reasons you should stop multitasking & actually get things done. (2015, December 1). 15Five. https://www.15five.com/blog/7-reasons-you-should-stop-multitasking/

REFERENCES

30 Best GARY KELLER Quotes of 34. (n.d.). The Cite Site. Retrieved October 25, 2022, from https://thecitesite.com/authors/gary-keller/

Trafft Team. (2020, May 28). *How poor time management can make your business suffer.* Trafft. https://trafft.com/poor-time-management/

UNC Kenan-Flagler Business School. (2020, October 5). *A benefit of multitasking.* The Well. https://thewell.unc.edu/2020/10/05/need-a-creativity-boost/

University of Southern California. (2018, July 17). *To multitask or not to multitask.* USC MAPP Online. https://appliedpsychologydegree.usc.edu/blog/to-multi task-or-not-to-multitask/

Why self-care matters in the workplace. (2017, November 15). LifeWorks Canada. https://wellbeing.lifeworks.com/ca/blog/self-care-matters-workplace/